Vintage Gifts to Knit

—— by Susan Crawford ——

Arbour House
Publishing

Arbour House Publishing

www.arbourhousepublishing.com

Dear Reader,

I have long been a fan and an avid collector of knitting and craft magazines from the first half of the Twentieth Century. Amongst my particular favourites are Stitchcraft and Needlework Illustrated, which together  provided the inspiration and the visual style for this book. Throughout the 30s, 40s and 50s, gift knitting or knitting for others, was an enormous part of being a knitter; with women usually knitting for all of her immediate family from necessity and knitting for others for economy. Whilst most of us are now fortunate enough to be able to choose what to knit, I hope the patterns in this book will inspire you with ideas when knitting for others and also tempt you to make time to knit some of them for yourselves!

Susan Crawford

First Published in 2010 by
Arbour House Publishing
Southport, UK
www.arbourhousepublishing.com

Photography: Susan Crawford & Charlie Moon
Illustration & Design: Gavin Crawford
Additional knitting: Dorothy Crawford
Models: Charlie Moon, Vickie Laverty, Gavin Crawford.

British Library Cataloguing-in-Publication Data
A catalogue record for this book is available from the British Library

ISBN 978-0-9556206-1-4

Printed and bound in the UK

R03-100920

This book can be purchased directly from: www.arbourhousepublishing.com

Vintage Gifts to Knit

by Susan Crawford

Contents

Arbour House Publishing

www.arbourhousepublishing.com

Miss Charlotte Moon, the well known model, finds wearing our colourful jersey such great fun even while doing the household chores. — Instruction for knitting it are on the facing page.

The Perfect Christmas Jumper

This delightful jumper with decorative reindeer motif is just what every girl needs for the festive season!

This pattern uses a combination of both Fair Isle and intarsia techniques. Charts A, B and D are worked in Fair Isle. Chart C however, uses both Fair Isle and Intarsia. Further information on how to work Chart C is given below. It is advisable to work the chart as suggested otherwise the main colour will show through the reindeer bodies! Also please note, there are two Chart C's, one for the first three sizes and one for the last three sizes. Please make sure you use the correct chart.

Shoulder seams are worked using a combination of short row shaping and three needle bind off. Where w&t is indicated on the shoulder seams, work the wrap and turn on the RS by slipping the stitch purlwise, bringing yarn forward, slipping stitch back onto left needle, taking yarn to back and turning work. On the WS of the work, the stitch is slipped in the same way but the yarn is taken first to the back and then forward.

Three needle bind off is worked on shoulder stitches placed back on straight needles with WS together. Use the third straight needle to knit first stitch from front needle together with first stitch from back needle. Repeat then BO first stitch. Repeat this process until all stitches are bound off.

MATERIALS

Jamieson & Smith 2 Ply Jumper Weight Yarn (100% Shetland wool) – knits up as a 4 ply (fingering weight) yarn (115 m/125 yds per 25 gm ball)
Main Colour – shade 125 – 10 (10, 11, 11, 12, 13) balls
Contrast Colour – shade 1 – 1(1, 1, 1, 2, 2) balls
4 Buttons
2.75 mm (US 2) straight needles
3.25 mm (US 4) straight needles (+ an extra needle for three needle bind off)
2.75 mm (US 2) circular needle
Stitch holders

TENSION

28 sts & 36 rows to 10 cm (4 inches) using 3.25 mm (US 4) needles over stocking stitch
31 sts & 34 rows to 10 cm (4 inches) using 3.25 mm (US 4) needles over Fair Isle pattern

To Fit						
in	28–30	32–34	36–38	40–42	44–46	48–50
cm	71–76	81–86	91–96	101–107	112–117	122–127
Actual Size						
in	32	36	39	44	47	51
cm	82	91	98	114	120	128
Length to underarm						
in	12.5	12.5	13.5	13.5	14.5	15
cm	31	31	34	34	37	38
Finished Length						
in	20	20	21	21.5	23	24
cm	51	51	53.5	54.5	58.5	61

Beginning with the front CO 115 (127,137, 159, 169, 179) sts, using MC and 2.75 mm (US 2) needles.

First Row (RS): * K1, P1, rep from * to last st, K1.
Second Row: * P1, K1, rep from * to last st, P1.
Repeat these two rows until work measures 8 cm (3.25 inches).
Change to 3.25 mm (US 4) needles and beginning with a knit row work 4 (4, 8, 8, 4, 8) rows in stocking stitch, ending with RS facing.
** **Next Row**: K15 (5,10, 5, 10, 15), work row 1 from chart A, (5, 7, 7, 9, 9, 9 times), K20 (10, 15, 10, 15, 20) in MC. This sets position of pattern. Continue following chart A, until all 12 rows have been worked. Work 2 rows in MC in stocking stitch.
Next Row: K15 (5,10, 5, 10, 15), work row 1 from chart B (5, 7, 7, 9, 9, 9 times), K5 in MC, K1 in CC, K14 (9, 9, 4, 9, 14) in MC. Continue working all 5 rows of Chart B working an extra small motif at the end of the row as set on first row above.
Commencing with a purl row and using MC, work 3 (3, 5, 5, 3, 3) rows in stocking stitch ***
Repeat from ** to *** twice (twice, twice, twice, three times, three times) more.
Next row (RS): K18 (24, 29, 35, 40, 45), work row 1 from chart C, K18 (24, 29, 35, 40, 45).

PLEASE NOTE REINDEER BODY IS WORKED IN INTARSIA WHILST LEGS AND ANTLERS ARE WORKED IN FAIRISLE – BUT USING SEPARATE BALLS OF CC FOR EACH MAIN AREA. THE CHRISTMAS TREE IN THE CENTRE IS WORKED IN FAIRISLE BUT USING A SEPARATE SMALL BALL OF CC. MC IS NOT CARRIED

ACROSS THE BODY OF THE REINDEER SO ADDITIONAL SMALL BALLS OF MC WILL BE REQUIRED AT THIS POINT.

Continue following Chart C until completed, and at the same time commence armhole shaping after 6 rows of Chart C have been worked as follows:
BO 2 (3, 3, 3, 3, 3) sts at beg of this row and foll 3 (5, 5, 5, 5, 5) rows (107, 109, 119, 141, 151, 161 sts).
Work 2 sts tog at each end of next 10 (11, 11, 13, 13, 15) rows (87, 87, 97, 115, 125, 131 sts).

On completion of Chart C, work 3 rows in stocking stitch using MC, ending with a RS row.

Next row: P36 (36, 39, 47, 50, 53), P2tog, place next 49(49, 56, 66, 73, 76) sts on to a stitch holder, turn, and work on rem 37 (37, 40, 48, 51, 54) sts only.
Work 2 sts tog on neck edge of each row until 27 (27, 27, 30, 33, 36) sts rem. Work a further 10 (10, 9, 6, 8, 8) rows without shaping.

SHOULDER SHAPING
K18 (18, 18, 20, 22, 24), w&t, purl to end, K9 (9, 9, 10, 11, 12), w&t, purl to end, knit across all stitches knitting wrapped stitch and wrap together by picking up wrap and knitting together with knit stitch on LH needle. Place these sts on a stitch holder. Commencing at opposite side edge, place 38 (38, 41, 49, 52, 55) sts on to needle and leave centre 11 (11,15, 17, 21, 21) sts on stitch holder. Work to match right front reversing all sts.

BACK
CO 115 (127,137, 159, 169, 179) sts, using MC and 2.75 mm (US 2) needles.
First Row (RS): * K1, P1, rep from * to last st, K1.
Second Row: * P1, K1, rep from * to last st, P1.
Repeat these two rows until work measures 8 cm (3.25 inches).
Change to 3.25 mm (US 4) needles and beginning with a knit row work without further shaping until back measures same as front to beginning of armhole shaping.

SHAPE ARMHOLE
BO 2 (3, 3, 3, 3, 3) sts at beg of this row and foll 3 (5, 5, 5, 5, 5) rows (107, 109, 119, 141, 151, 161 sts).
Work 2 sts tog at each end of next 10 (11, 11, 13, 13, 15) rows (87, 87, 97, 115, 125, 131 sts).

Continue without shaping until work measures 10 cm (4 inches) less than front to start of shoulder shaping, then divide for centre back opening as follows:

Next row (RS): K42 (42, 47, 56, 61, 64), K2tog, K to end. Turn, and work on first 43 (43, 48, 57, 62, 65) sts only. Place rem sts onto a stitch holder.

Row 1: Purl to last 4 sts., (K1, P1) twice.

Row 2: (P1, K1) twice, knit to end.

These two rows set button band sts. After a further 4 rows have been worked, make buttonhole as follows:

Next row: Patt 2, BO 1, patt to end.

Next row: Patt to BO st., turn, CO 1, bringing yarn forward before placing CO st onto LH needle, patt to end.

Repeat these 8 rows twice more, then rows 1 and 2 twice more, and finally work row 1 only, once more, ending with RS facing.

Work shoulder as for front. Join shoulder stitches to corresponding front shoulder stitches using three needle bind off method. (See pattern notes) Leave rem 16 (16, 21, 27, 29, 29) sts on stitch holder for back neck. Rejoin yarn to rem sts with WS facing. CO 4 sts.

Row 1: (P1, K1), purl to end.

Row 2: Knit to last 4 sts, (K1, P1) twice.

These 2 rows set pattern. Repeat these two rows a further 14 times each.

Work shoulder to match first side reversing shapings, work three needle bind off as before and leave rem 20 (20, 25, 31, 33, 33) sts on holder for back neck.

SLEEVES

Using 2.75 mm (US 2) needles and MC, CO 60 (60, 60, 64, 64, 70) sts.

Next row: *K1, P1, rep from * to end. Repeat this row 28 times more. Work one more row in rib, increasing 1 st at the end of the row. (61, 61, 61, 65, 65, 71) sts)

Change to 3.25 mm (US 4) needles and commencing with a knit row work in stocking stitch, increasing one stitch at each end of every 8th row until 87 (87, 87, 93, 99, 105) sts. Work without further shaping until sleeve measures 48 cm (19 inches) or required length.

SHAPE SLEEVE HEAD

BO 4 sts at beg of next 6 rows. (63, 63, 63, 69, 75, 81 sts)

Next row (RS): K13 (13, 13, 16, 19, 22), work row 1 of Chart D, K13 (13, 13, 16, 19, 22). Work 2 repeats of Chart D taking care to work highlighted motif once only (See images for clarification). Work 3 rows in stocking stitch.

BO 21 (21, 21, 23, 25, 27) sts at the beg of the next rows. 21 (21, 21, 23, 25, 27) sts rem. Work 16 (16, 16, 18, 20, 22) further rows without shaping ending with a WS row. BO rem sts.

NECKBAND

With RS facing, commencing at left back and using 2.75 mm (US 2) circular needle, patt 4 sts in moss st for border, knit across 12 (12, 17, 23, 25, 25) sts, pick up 5 sts up left back neck, 24 (24, 26, 28, 30, 32) sts down left side front, knit across 11 (11, 15, 17, 21, 21) sts on centre front KNITTING TOGETHER CENTRE 2 STS, pick up 24 (24, 26, 28, 30, 32) sts up right side front, 5 sts down right back neck, knit across 16 (16, 21, 27, 29, 29) sts across back neck, and then patt across rem 4 sts in moss st for border (104, 104, 122, 140, 152, 156 sts). Work 1 (1, 1, 3, 3, 3) row(s) in moss st.

Next row: Patt 2, BO 1 st, continue in moss st to end of row.

Next row: Moss st to BO sts, turn, CO 1 bringing yarn forward before placing CO st onto LH needle, moss st to end.

Work in moss st for 2 more rows. BO in pattern.

MAKING UP

Darn in all ends. Block pieces, taking care not to press ribs. Create box sleeve by joining CO sts at top of sleeve to side seam of 16 (16, 16, 18, 20, 22) rows worked straight (See diagram below).

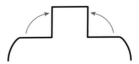 Place a pin at the centre top of the sleeve head and match this point to the corresponding shoulder seam – with RS together – and pin in place. Pin BO edges of sleeve and body together, pin remainder of seam together easing in any excess fabric. Once

This winter woolly is perfect for casual wear

pinned correctly join seams together using a neat back stitch. Repeat with second sleeve.

Either ... With RS together, pin side and sleeve seams together matching ribs and underarm seams. Sew together with a neat back stitch from top of body rib to top of sleeve rib, leaving a long tail at beginning sufficient to sew rib seam. Flatten out cuff and slip stitch rib seam together. Thread needle to long tail at other end and repeat process with body ribbing.

Or... Pin seams together at underarm and at top of ribbings with WS together. Sew seam together using mattress stitch from top of body rib to top of sleeve rib, leaving a long tail at beginning sufficient to sew rib seam. Flatten out cuff and slip stitch rib seam together. Thread needle to long tail at other end and repeat process with body ribbing.

Darn in remaining ends. Sew buttons in place.

Chart A

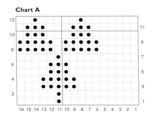

Key
☐ MC (Main Colour)
⊡ CC (Contrast Colour)

Chart B

Chart D Repeat chart twice but work highlighted motif once only

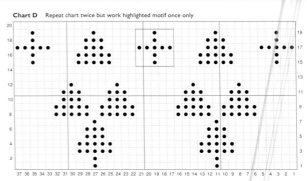

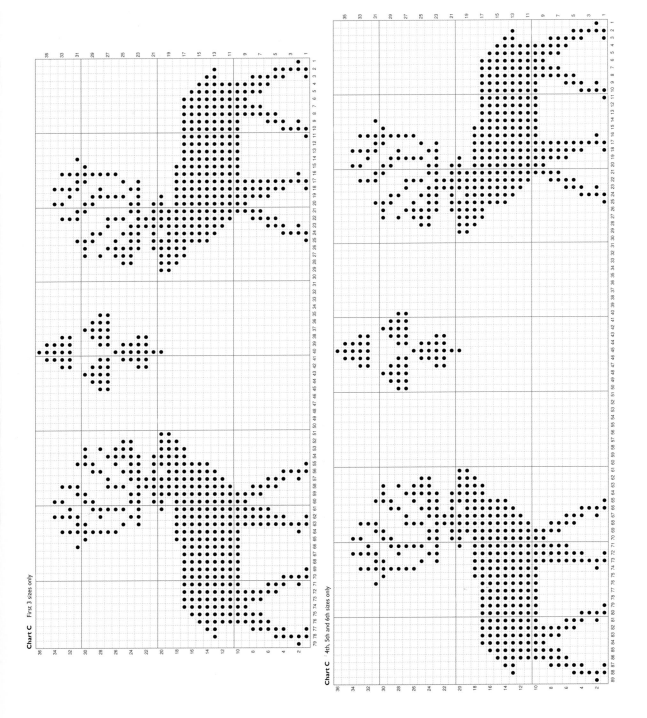

Chart C First 3 sizes only

Chart C 4th, 5th and 6th sizes only

9

This adorable set is as soft as a hug
and with its clever slip stitch pattern looks just like a kiss.

Hugs and Kisses

*This feminine little trio
will keep you snuggly and warm
yet stylish right through to spring!*

TENSION

24 sts to 10 cm (4 inches) using 3.5 mm (US 5) needles over stocking stitch – using MC

For Scarf: 26 sts x 44 rows using 3.75 mm (US 5) needles over stitch pattern

For Mitts & Bonnet: 30 sts x 50 rows using 3.25 mm (US 4) needles over stitch pattern

MATERIALS

Du Store Alpakka Babysilk (80% alpaca, 20% silk) yarn (133 m per 50 gm ball) – this is a 4 ply (fingering weight) Main Colour – shade 313 – 4 (5, 5) balls for set [2 (3, 3) balls for scarf, 1 ball each for gloves and bonnet] Garn Studios Drops Alpaca (100% alpaca) yarn (180 m / 200 yds per 50 gm ball) Contrast Colour – shade 1101 – 3 balls (Just over 1 ball for hat and also for scarf, under 1 ball for mitts) 1 pair 3.75 mm (US 5) straight needles 1 pair 3.25 mm (US 4) straight needles 3.25 mm (US 4) circular needle Set of 3.75 mm (US 5) double pointed needles (dpns) 2 x 3.25 mm (US 4) double pointed needles (dpns) Safety pin

PATTERN

Row 1: Using MC throughout, * K2, SL 2 purlwise, rep from * to last 2 sts, K2.
Row 2: Using MC throughout, purl to end of row.
Row 3: * SL 2 purlwise, K2 using CC, rep from * to last 2 sts, SL 2 purlwise.
Row 4: Using CC throughout, purl to end of row.

PATTERN NOTES

The different parts of this set are worked on different needle sizes but using the same pattern to achieve different fabrics. This is quite deliberate, for example, to obtain a softer scarf and a firmer bonnet.

To fit sizes

Hat – Small: 11–13 years
Medium: small to medium adult
Large: large adult
(medium shown in photographs)

Scarf – 122 cm x 28.5 cm (48 inches x 11.25 inches) – child
152.5 cm x 32 cm (60 inches x 12.5 inches) – adult

Mitts – Small: 11–13 years
Medium: small to medium adult
Large: large adult
(medium shown in photographs)

Scarf

CO 76 (84) sts, using MC and 3.75 mm (US 5) needles. Work in moss st as folls:
Next row (RS): *K1, P1, rep from * to end.
Next row: *P1, K1, rep from * to end.

BEGIN PATTERN AS FOLLOWS

Next row: Work 5 sts in moss st, work row 1 of pattern, work 5 sts in moss st.

This sets the pattern, working a moss st border in MC over entire length of scarf. On the first working of row 3 of pattern a second ball of MC needs to be introduced after main pattern is worked to knit moss st border at end of row.

Continue working 4 rows of pattern until scarf measures approx 119 (150) cm (47, 59 inches) ending with row 2. Using MC only, work 6 rows of moss st. BO, taking care not to make bind off too tight.

MAKING UP

Darn in all ends. Block and press scarf.

Dutch Bonnet

Starting at back of head, CO 23 (27, 27) sts with one strand each of MC and CC and using 3.75 mm (US 5) needles. Commencing with a K row, work in stocking stitch, inc 1 st at each end of 7th (9th, 11th) and every foll 6th (8th, 8th) row until 31 (35, 35) sts. Work 3 rows without shaping, then commence decreases as folls:

Dec 1 st at beg of next 4 rows 27 (31, 31) sts, BO 2 sts at beg of foll 2 rows (23, 27, 27 sts), BO 3 sts at beg of foll 3 rows (14, 18, 18 sts), then finally dec 1 st at beg of foll 2 rows (12, 16, 16 sts). BO rem sts.

With RS facing, using 3.25 mm (US 4) circular needle and MC only, start at lower edge and pick up 31 (35,

39) sts up first side of back panel, 48 sts across shaped top and 31 (35, 39) sts down other side (110, 118, 126 sts).

Next row: Purl.

**Work in main pattern commencing with row 1 and increasing at each end of the 7th and every following 6th row (4, 4, 5 times) 118 (126, 136 sts). Continue without further shaping until brim measures approx 13 (13, 15) cm (5, 5, 6 inches) ending with row 4. Using MC only, purl next two rows. (Seam line) Change to CC and work without shaping for 18 (18, 22) rows. Commence shaping to match brim by dec 1 st at each end of next and foll 6th row (4, 4, 5 times). BO all sts.

MAKING UP

With bonnet flat, block and press firmly. Fold brim in half at seam line and pin facing in place along picked up stitches. Ease in excess fabric along length. When happy with fit, slip stitch into place using CC taking care not to got through to RS of bonnet with stitches.

If possible, place on a head form and steam gently in position. Alternatively, place bonnet on a ball or stuff with newspaper or similar to create shape and then steam gently.

Mitts

Please note: Due to nature of the two contrasting stitches these mitts are worked in two pieces.

RIGHT HAND MITT

Starting with the back of mitt, CO 26 (30, 34) sts using 3.25 mm (US 4) needles and MC.

Commencing with row 1, work in stitch pattern until mitt measures 15 (18, 20) cm (6, 7, 8 inches) or required length to tip of little finger, ending with a RS row.

Shape top whilst continuing in pattern as folls:

P2tog at each end of next and every foll purl row until 12 (16, 16) sts rem. BO in MC.

To make palm of mitt, CO 21 (23, 25) sts, with one strand each of MC and CC and using 3.75 mm (US 5) needles. Commencing with a knit row work in stocking stitch until work measures 7.5 (10, 11.5) cm (3, 4, 4.5 inches) ending with a WS row.

THUMB PLACEMENT

Next row: K2, K next 7 (8, 8) sts and leave on a safety pin, K 12 (13, 15).

Next row: Purl to sts on pin, turn and CO 7 (8, 8) sts, turn and P to end.

Continue in stocking stitch until palm measures 15 (18, 20) cm (6, 7, 8 inches) or desired length as for back of mitt, ending with a WS row.

Shape top by K2tog at each end of next and every foll knit row until 11 (13, 13) sts rem. Purl one row. BO rem sts.

TO WORK THUMB

Using 3.75 mm (US 5) dpns and one strand each of MC and CC, pick up 8 (9, 9) sts across CO edge of thumb, K7 (8, 8) sts off pin and pick up additional st at end (16, 18, 18 sts in total).

Next row: K6 (7, 7) K2tog, K6 (7, 7), K2tog.
Knit for 13 (15, 17) rounds, or for desired length.

TO SHAPE THUMB

Next round: * K2tog, K3 (4, 4), K2tog, rep from * once more.

Leaving 5 (6, 6) sts on each needle and ensuring they are correctly distributed between front and back of thumb, graft these sts together.

LEFT HAND MITT

Work exactly as for right hand mitt, except when placing thumb, work row as folls:

Next row: K12 (13, 15), K next 7 (8, 8) sts and leave on a safety pin, K2.

MAKING UP

Darn in all ends. Block and press firmly. With WS together pin palm and back of mitts together. Using MC work a neat backstitch close to the edge of the work and directly under BO edge (as shown in photos) to create ridge.

I CORD BINDING

CO 3 sts, using MC and 3.25 mm (US 4) dpns. Knit 3 sts, DO NOT TURN WORK, push sts to right hand end of needle, pull yarn across back of sts firmly, knit 3 sts again. Repeat this process until cord is long enough when slightly stretched to fit round CO edge of mitt with a very slight over lap. (Commence at thumb edge of palm) Leave on needle and pin around bottom edge of mitt. If fits correctly BO sts leaving long tail. Overlap BO sts over CO sts, pin and then neatly sew cord in place around edge. Repeat with 2nd mitt.

*Our model, Miss Victoria Laverty, pictured above
is well wrapped up against the winter's chill.*

*Try knitting these boldly patterned gloves
in different colours to match your outfits!*

Elegant Coat-Gloves

*Stylish yet practical – perfect
for town and country walks!*

D ue to the nature of the pattern on the palm of
these gloves, they are knitted flat on straight
needles rather than on dpns, with a side seam. If
preferred, the fingers and thumb can be knitted in the
round on dpns without any difficulty. The gloves are
designed to be worn quite far down the lower arm
to prevent gaps appearing between the end of the
glove and the cuff of the coat. Contrast colours B and
C only require a very small amount of yarn and
oddments could be used for these. Please note, that
although the gloves are knitted in fair isle, the
contrast colours B and C are not carried across the
palm of the glove, also the main motif uses three
colours to a row rather than the traditional two
colours. The gloves can be made shorter in the hand
by reducing number of rows worked between rows
1 and 6 and 46 and 51 of chart A, even deleting this
section altogether or alternatively deleting rows 8 to
10 and 42 to 44. The hand can be made longer by
working additional plain rows after rows 7, 11, 42 and
45. The same number of rows would have to be
added or subtracted from chart B. Smaller or larger
needles can also be used to alter finished size of
gloves.

Wondering how to get the finger length on your
gloves just right? Before starting to knit, place each
hand on a piece of paper with fingers apart and draw
round. Use this as a template for your glove as you
work.

To fit average ladies hand
Palm length to thumb gusset (without ribbing) 11 cm (4.5 inches)

Width around glove, measured around hand immediately above
thumb gusset 18.5 cm (7.5 inches).

MATERIALS

Jamieson & Smith 2 ply Jumper Weight Yarn (100%
Shetland wool) – knits up as a 4 ply (fingering
weight) yarn (115 m / 125 yds per 25 gm ball)
Main Colour (MC) – shade 202 (natural) – 2 balls
Contrast Colour A – shade 21 (Navy blue) – 1 ball
Contrast Colour B – shade 34 (Emerald green) – 1 ball
Contrast Colour C – shade 9097 (Deep red) – 1 ball
1 pair 2.25 mm (US 1) straight needles
Stitch markers

TENSION

38 sts & 32 rows to 10 cm (4 inches) over fair isle
pattern using 2.25 mm (US 1) needles

RIGHT GLOVE

CO 56 sts using MC and 2.25 mm (US 1) needles.

Row 1 (RS): *K2, P2, rep from * to end.

Repeat this row until work measures 7.5 cm (3 inches) ending with WS facing.

Next row: (Rib 10, inc 1) 5 times, P1 (61 sts).

From this point the glove is worked in stocking stitch commencing with a knit row.

Next row (RS): This row sets position of charts – work row 1 of chart A across first 31 sts, then work row 1 of chart B across rem 30 sts.

Next row: work row 2 of chart B followed by chart A.

Continue in this manner until 10 rows in all have been worked.

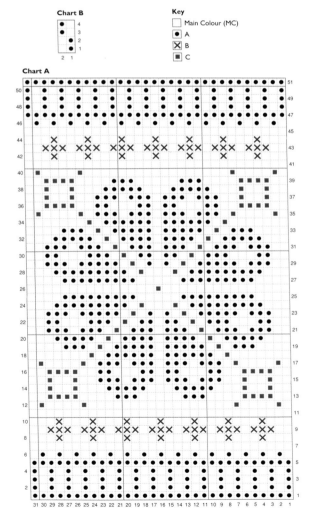

Chart B

Key
- ☐ Main Colour (MC)
- ● A
- ✕ B
- ■ C

Chart A

THUMB PLACEMENT

Next row: K 31 sts from row 11 of chart A, using MC - PM (K1, M1) twice, PM. You will now need to join in a 2nd ball of shade A, then work 28 sts from chart B.

Work 3 more rows, without any further increases, working the 4 sts between the markers in MC at all times.

Continue working from charts A and B, increase on every 3rd row, (6 times) after first and before last sts within markers, until 16 sts between markers.

Continue in pattern across all sts until work measures 16.5 cm (6.5 inches) from CO edge, or required length to thumb gusset.

Next Row: Patt 31 sts, SM, K16, turn

Next Row: P16, turn and CO 6 sts.

Continue in st st on these 22 sts only for 22 rows or for required thumb length.

Next Row: (K2tog, K2) 5 times, K2tog.

Next Row: Purl.

Next Row: (K2tog, K2) 4 times.

Break off wool, leaving end long enough to draw through sts tightly and stitch down length of thumb.

With RS facing and using MC pick up 7 sts at the base of the thumb, work in pattern to end of row. (66 sts). Continue in pattern (including 7 sts at base of thumb) until Charts A and B have been completed.

Next Row: Using MC only, P3 (P2tog, P7) 7 times (59 sts).

Use MC only from this point to complete fingers.

1ST FINGER

K38, turn P17, turn, CO 3 sts, K20.

Continue on these 20 sts for 27 rows or required length.

Next Row: (K2tog, K2) 5 times.

Next Row: Purl.

Next Row: (K2tog, K2) 3 times, K2tog, K1.

Next Row: (P2tog, P1) 3 times, P2tog.

Complete as thumb.

2ND FINGER

With RS facing, pick up 3 sts from cast on edge of 1st finger, K7, from left hand needle, turn, P17, turn, CO 3 sts, K20.

Continue on these 20 sts for 29 rows or for required length.
Complete as 1st finger.

3RD FINGER
Working 27 rows instead of 29, work as for 2nd finger.

4TH FINGER
With RS facing, pick up 3 sts from cast on edge of 3rd finger, K7, from left hand needle, turn, P17.
Continue on these 17 sts for 22 rows or for required length.
Next Row: (K2tog, K2) 4 times, K1.
Next Row: P.
Next Row: (K2tog, K2) 3 times, K1.
Complete as 1st finger, leaving enough yarn to also sew together side seam.

LEFT GLOVE
CO 56 sts using MC and 2.25 mm (US 1) needles.
Row 1 (RS): *K2, P2, rep from * to end.
Repeat this row until work measures 7.5 cm (3 inches) ending with WS facing.
Next row: (Rib 10, inc 1) 5 times, P1 (61 sts).
From this point the glove is worked in stocking stitch commencing with a knit row.
Next row (RS): This row sets position of charts — work row 1 of chart B across first 30 sts, then work row 1 of chart A across rem 31 sts.
Next row: work row 2 of chart A followed by chart B. Continue in this manner until 10 rows in all have been worked.

THUMB PLACEMENT
Next row: K 28 sts from row 11 of chart B, using MC – PM (K1, M1) twice, PM. You will now need to join in a 2nd ball of shade A, then work 31 sts from chart A.
Work 3 more rows, without any further increases, working the 4 sts between the markers in MC at all times.
Continue working from charts A and B, increase on every 3rd row, (6 times) after first and before last sts within markers, until 16 sts between markers.
Continue in pattern across all sts until work measures 16.5 cm (6.5 inches) or required length to thumb gusset.

Next Row: Patt 28 sts, SM, K16, turn
Next Row: P16, turn and CO 6 sts.
Continue in st st on these 22 sts for 21 rows or required thumb length.
Next Row: (K2tog, K2) 5 times, K2tog.
Next Row: Purl.
Next Row: (K2tog, K2) 4 times.
Break off wool, leaving end long enough to draw through sts tightly and stitch down length of thumb and side seam.

Work fingers as for Right Glove.

MAKING UP
Sew up remaining seams and darn in all ends.

Knit a pair of these colourful fair isle gloves for all your friends!

*This dashing motoring hood is perfect
for weekend trips in the motor car and is
also stylish enough to be worn round town!*

Miss Laverty's Motoring Hood

This is a simple pattern suitable for beginner knitters. The pixie hood is knitted separately with shaping added at the centre back for a more comfortable fit. The front of the scarf is folded back and the scarf is then sewn in place over the bottom seam. The scarf can easily be made longer to suit personal taste but more yarn will be needed.

Such a simple project, perfect for the new knitter.

Finished Size
Scarf length 102 cm (40 inches)
Hood length 48 cm (19 inches)
Hood depth (not including folded-over edge)
18 cm (7 inches)

MATERIALS

Berroco Ultra Alpaca Light (50% Alpaca, 50% Peruvian Wool) (133 m/144 yds per 50 gm skein) – knits up as a 4 ply (fingering weight)
4 skeins shade 4245 (black)
1 pair 3.75 mm (US 5) straight needles
2 detachable stitch markers or waste yarn

TENSION

23 sts & 32 rows to 10 cm (4 inches) using 3.75 mm (US 5) needles over stocking stitch
32 sts & 32 rows to 10 cm (4 inches) using 3.75 mm (US 5) needles over single rib (unstretched).

The North wind will blow and you may have snow, but this charming hood will keep you warm where-ever you may go!

PIXIE HOOD

Using 3.75 mm (US 5) needles, CO 68 sts.
Row 1: * K1, P1, rep from * to end.
Keeping continuity of rib pattern, increase one st at beg of every 4th row until 72 sts, PM at point where last increase st worked.

Continue without further shaping until work measures 43 cm (17 inches) from the cast on edge. PM at commencement of next row and patt 2 sts tog at beg of this row and every foll 4th row until 68 sts rem. Work 3 rows without shaping. Bind off slightly loosely in rib.

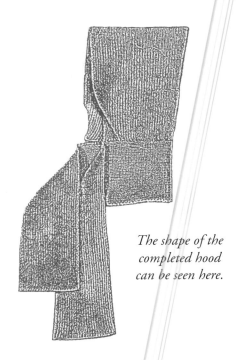

The shape of the completed hood can be seen here.

SCARF

Using 3.75 mm (US 5) needles, CO 51 sts.
Row 1: K1, *P1, K1, rep from * to end.
Row 2: P1, *K1, P1, rep from * to end.

Repeat these 2 rows until work measures 102 cm (40 inches) or required length. Bind off slightly loosely in rib.

MAKING UP

Fold the hood placing markers together. These two edges to the point at the top, form the back seam on the hood. With RS together sew up back seam. On lower front of hood fold back each edge approx 4 cm (1.5 inches) on RS of work and pin in place. Fold scarf in half lengthwise and place a pin to mark centre back. Match centre back of scarf to back seam of hood. Pin scarf in place over hood and over folded back edges. Stretch scarf slightly as you do this. Once you are happy that the two scarf lengths are equal, sew scarf to hood through all layers. Darn in any ends. There is no need to press.

Spring is in the air when you use this colourful tea cosy to keep your favourite brew warm!

Flower-ty Pot

*Choose colours that
complement your kitchen.*

The under-cosy is knitted in two separate pieces which are then joined together around the spout and handle. The petals are knitted individually and then positioned and sewn into place over the under-cosy. This is a simple knit which requires some sewing skills and patience. With up to four layers of wool around your tea pot this cosy provides excellent insulation.

MATERIALS

Jamieson & Smith 2 Ply Jumper Weight Yarn (100% shetland wool) – knits up as a 4 ply (fingering weight) yarn (115 m/125 yds per 25 gm ball) Main Colour - shade 141 3 balls Contrast Colour A – shade 070 – 1 ball Contrast Colour B – shade 001 – 1 ball 1 button 3.25 mm (US 4) straight needles

To fit a 6 cup tea pot

Tension
24 sts to 10 cm (4 inches) using 3.25 mm (US 4) needles over stocking stitch

UNDER-COSY (TWO SIDES ALIKE)

Using 3.25 mm (US 4) needles and MC, CO 60 sts.
Next row: *K1, P1, rep from * to end.
Repeat this row until work measures 4 cm (1.5 inches) from CO edge.
Commencing with a knit row, work in stocking stitch until work measures 10 cm (4 inches) from CO edge, ending with purl row.

TO SHAPE TOP

Row 1: *K8, K2tog, rep from * to end.
Work 3 rows.
Row 5: *K7, K2tog, rep from * to end.
Work 3 rows.
Row 9: *K6, K2tog, rep from * to end.
Work 3 rows.
Row 13: *K5, K2tog, rep from * to end.
Work 3 rows.
Row 17: *K4, K2tog, rep from * to end.
Work 3 rows.
Row 21: *K3, K2tog, rep from * to end.

From this point on, work a single purl row only after each decrease row.
Row 23: *K2, K2tog, rep from * to end.
Row 25: *K1, K2tog, rep from * to end.
Row 27: K2tog across the row.
Next row: BO, purling 2sts tog along row as you do so.

PETALS

Make 16 petals in MC
12 petals in A and 10 petals in B

Using 3.25 mm (US 4) needles, CO 14 sts, leaving a long end at beg of CO row. Work in stocking stitch throughout.
Row 1 (WS): Purl.
Row 2: *K1, kfb of next st, rep from * to end of row (21 sts).
Patt 3 rows.
Row 6: K1, K2togtbl, K to last 3 sts, K2tog, K1.
Patt 3 rows.
Repeat last 4 rows twice more.

Row 18: As Row 6.
Row 19: Purl.
Repeat last 2 rows 4 times more
(5 sts remain).
Row 28: K1, SL1, K2tog., psso, K1.
Row 29: P3tog.
Break wool and draw end through
remaining loop.

Repeat until the correct number
of petals are made.

MAKING UP

Block each piece firmly. Place the 2 under-cosy
pieces together with RS facing and pin seams
leaving openings for tea pot spout and handle —
usually a larger opening for the handle. Try over your
tea pot and adjust to fit if necessary. Sew up seams.
Turn cosy right way out and place over tea pot. Using
the photos as a guide and beginning with petals in
shade B at the highest point on the cosy, pin petals
into place. Continue layering with shade A petals, then
finally MC petals until happy with layout. Leave all
petals on one side of cosy in
place as a guide and remove all
petals except for shade B on
the other side. Commence
sewing into place using long
end from CO row. If
necessary use remaining end
at point of petal to add a
supporting stitch through
layers, otherwise darn in
these ends as you go along.
Re-pin second layer of
petals and continue in the
same manner until all petals
are sewn in place. Repeat
process on other side.
From the inside of the
cosy, sew a button in place
at the very centre top of
the cosy.

When finished, put the kettle on!

When the world is all at odds
And the mind is all at sea
Then cease the useless tedium
And brew a cup of tea.
There is magic in its' fragrance,
There is solace in its' taste;

And the laden moments vanish
Somehow into space.
And the world becomes a lovely thing!
There's beauty as you'll see;
All because you briefly stopped
To brew a cup of tea.

William Gladstone

Our delightful model is all ready for a busy day in the city.

This pretty, cropped cape is the perfect cover up in the spring time, adding a touch of sophistication to every young lady's daytime wardrobe. Knitted in this fascinating tufted stitch it is a fun and quick knit. Shown here in an elegant soft green and classic black combination, you can knit this little cape in colour mixes to complement your wardrobe.

To fit sizes			
	S	M	L
	30–36 in	38–44 in	46–52 in
	76–92 cm	96–112 cm	117–132 cm
Finished Length*	10 in	10.75 in	11.5 in
	25.5 cm	27.5 cm	29 cm
Width	60 in	64 in	68 in
(at widest point)	152.5 cm	162.5 cm	172 cm

Our model is photographed wearing a small size cape in the short length.

* See pattern notes.

MATERIALS

Biggan Design DK (8 ply) First Cross Merino Wool (105 m/115 yds per 50gm ball)
5 (5, 6) balls shade 495 (Green/MC)
1 ball shade 000 (Black/CC)
4 mm (US 6) needles
5 mm (US 8) needles
1 button

TENSION

2.5 pattern repeats = 5cm (2 in)
and 5 rows = 2.5 cm (1 in)

Town & City Tufted Cape

for the 'London Girl' look

PATTERN NOTES
To make tuft
(K1, P1, K1) all into front of next stitch – referred to throughout the pattern as T1

Please note, the cape is worked from the top down. Stitch count fluctuates on different rows of the pattern, so be careful to only check your stitch count on the appropriate row.

The finished length is measured from the top of the main body at the front neck and includes the garter stitch edging around the bottom of the cape. The cape is very generous and accommodating in size and shape and will fit a variety of sizes. As a result, I suggest you consider what fit you would like before choosing your size. The small will actually fit a 42 inch chest but it will fit higher and more open at the front.

If you would prefer a longer length cape repeat from ** to *** an additional 3 times for a cape approximately 35.5 cm (14 in) in length. Remember to work the front pieces to match the back.

BACK

CO 35 (39, 43) sts using 5 mm (US 8) needles and MC.

Row 1 (WS): K1, *T1, P3tog, rep from * to last 2 sts, T1, K1. (The knit stitches at either end of the row are selvedge stitches.) 37 (41, 45) sts.

Row 2 and all even numbered rows (RS): K1, P to last st, K1.

Row 3: K1, T1, P2tog, *T1, P3tog, rep from * to last 5 sts, T1, P2tog, T1, K1 (41, 45, 49 sts).

Repeat last 2 rows until a total of 60 (64, 68) rows have been worked (153, 165, 177 sts).

** **Next row**: K1, * P3tog, T1, rep from * to last 4 sts, P3tog, K1.

Next row: as row 2.

Next row: K1, *T1, P3tog, rep from * to last 2 sts, T1, K1.

Next row: as row 2 ***

Rep from ** to *** once more.

LOWER EDGE SHAPING

Next row: K1, *P3tog, T1, rep from * to last 17 (21, 25) sts, turn, pattern to last 17 (21, 25) sts, turn, pattern to last 34 (42, 50) sts, turn, patt to last 34 (42, 50) sts. Leave to one side.

LEFT FRONT
(COMMENCES AT SHOULDER)

CO 1 st using 5 mm needles and MC.

Row 1 (WS): T1 (3 sts).

Row 2 (RS): K1, P1, KFB (4 sts).

Row 3: (Place marker or waste yarn here to denote side edge) T1, P2tog, K1 (5 sts).

Row 4: K1, P3, KFB (6 sts).

Row 5: K1, T1, P2tog, T1, K1 (9 sts).

Row 6 and all even numbered rows: K1, P to last st, K1.

Row 7: K1, (T1, P2tog) twice, T1, K1 (13 sts).

Row 9: K1, T1, P2tog, T1, P3tog T1, P2tog, T1, K1 (17 sts).

Row 11: K1, T1, P2tog, *T1, P3tog, rep from * to last st, T1, turn, CO 5 sts for front neck (25 sts).

Row 13: As row 11 (33 sts).

Row 15: K1, T1, P2tog, *T1, P3tog, rep from * to last st, K1. (34 sts)

Row 16: as row 6.

This feminine winged collar adds just the right touch of sophistication.

Row 17: K1, T1, P2tog, *T1, P3tog, rep from * to last 2 sts, T1, K1 (37 sts).

Row 18: as row 6.

Repeat last 4 rows until 81 (85, 89) sts. Continue in pattern without increasing – instead of working P2tog at beginning of rows 15 and 17, work P3tog – until 67 (71, 75) rows have been worked.

Next row: Pattern to last 17 (21, 25) sts, turn, patt to end, turn, patt to last 33 (41, 49) sts, turn, patt to end.

Leave to one side.

RIGHT FRONT (COMMENCES AT SHOULDER)

Work as for left front reversing all shapings commencing as follows:

Row 1 (WS): T1 (3 sts).

Row 2 (RS): KFB, K1, P1.

Row 3: K1, P2tog, T1 [place marker or waste yarn here to denote side edge] (5 sts).

EDGING

Join side seams carefully overlapping front edges over back selvedge seams and stitching at back of work and place all stitches onto one needle. Rejoin MC to one end of cape and with WS facing knit across all stitches. Change to CC and 4 mm (US 6) needles and work 4 more rows in garter stitch. Bind off.

BUTTON BAND

Using 4 mm (US 6) needles and CC, and with RS facing pick up and knit 66 (70, 74) sts evenly down left front edge.

Row 1 (WS): * P2, K2, rep from * to last 2 sts, P2.

Row 2: *K2, P2, rep from * to last 2 sts, K2.

Repeat these 2 rows 6 times more. BO in rib.

BUTTONHOLE BAND

Using 4 mm (US 6) needles and CC, and with RS facing pick up and knit 66 (70, 74) sts evenly up right front edge.

Row 1 (WS): * P2, K2, rep from * to last 2 sts, P2.

Row 2: *K2, P2, rep from * to last 2 sts, K2.

Repeat these 2 rows once more, then row 1 again.

Row 6 (RS): Patt to last 14 sts, BO 6 sts, patt to end.

Row 7: Patt to BO sts, turn and CO 7 sts, turn again and patt to end.

Row 8: Patt to last 15 sts, patt 2 tog, patt to end (66, 70, 74 sts).

Continue to match button band. BO in rib.

NECK BAND

Using 4 mm (US 6) needles and CC, and with RS facing pick up 9 sts across buttonhole band, 18 sts up right front, 26 (30, 34) sts across back, 18 sts down left front and 9 sts across button band (80, 84, 88 sts). Change to 5 mm (US 8) needles and work 6 rows in garter stitch. BO.

MAKING UP

Darn in all ends. Press firmly on wrong side of cape carefully setting required shape. Pin and lightly press rib bands. Fold over edges of garter stitch neck band and stitch into place as shown. Sew on button.

Detail of tufted stitch.

33

Whether skating, shopping or at the office,
this flattering skirt fits perfectly in to every woman's wardrobe.

'The No Need to Skate'

Skating Skirt

This flirty skirt can be worn casually or formally. Worked in 8 panels, it gently flares over the hips and swirls attractively just above the knee. Knitted in a firm wool for stretch but strength and with a decorative icelandic flower motif added for detail. This skirt can be customised for the perfect fit as explained in the pattern and can be worked with or without the motif detail, providing you with the perfect skirt for every occasion – not just for skating!

It is worked from the top down and can be adjusted to fit any waist size or skirt length. The pattern given is for a particular length and fit but it is very easy to make alterations to this by adding or subtracting rounds between increases or reducing/increasing the number of increases worked overall.

MATERIALS

Jamieson & Smith 2 ply Jumper Weight Yarn (100% Shetland wool) – knits up as a 4 ply (fingering weight) yarn (115 m/125 yds per 25 gm ball)
Main Colour (MC) – shade FC34 – 8 (9, 10) balls
Contrast Colour (CC) – shade 1 – 1 ball
3.25 mm (US 4) circular needle
A length of 2.5 cm (1 in) wide elastic
Sewing thread and needle

TENSION

25 sts & 36 rows = 10 cm (4 inches) using 3.25 mm (US 4) needles over stocking stitch worked in the round (every round knit).

Sizes				
To fit waist:		24–28 in	30 –34 in	36–40 in
		61–71 cm	76–86 cm	92–101 cm
Actual Size:		30 in	36 in	42 in
		76 cm	91 cm	104 cm

Finished Length: All Sizes 50 cm (19.75 in) to top of folded waistband

(size shown in photographs is a 30–34 inch waist)

WAISTBAND

CO 188 (228, 268) sts using 3.25 mm (US 4) circular needle and MC. Join into round, placing marker to indicate round end.

Knit 10 rounds.
Next round (RS): P.
Knit 10 rows.

SKIRT

Next round: Place markers for shaping (classing existing marker as left side seam) as follows: * K23 (29, 33), PM, K24 (28, 34) PM, K23 (29, 33) PM, K24 (28, 34) ** PM, repeat from * to **

Knit every round and at same time work 16 increases on next and every foll 15th row (4 times) as follows:
K1, M1, * K to within 1st of marker, M1, K1, SM, K1, M1, repeat to last st on round, M1, K1.
Continue until 268 (308, 348) sts.
Work 14 rounds without shaping.
Work increases as before but this time work

16 increases on next and every foll 8th row ** until 412 (452, 492) sts **AND AT THE SAME TIME** after 113 rounds worked from original placement of markers, work snowflake chart in the centre of first, third, fifth and seventh panels of skirt (Each snowflake is 29 sts in width).

** If you wish to make the skirt longer or shorter reduce or increase the number of rounds worked between increases from here, dividing additional or fewer rounds worked equally between each increase.

Use a separate small ball of CC for each section. To continue working in rounds it is necessary to break the yarn at the end of each motif and rejoin at the beginning of the next round as the yarn will be at the 'wrong end' of the motif. Alternatively introduce a 2nd circular needle and work backwards and forwards over these rows either knitting and purling or if you are familiar with the technique, knitting backwards as well as forwards.

After snowflake motifs completed continue in MC only until 148 rounds worked.
Purl 2 rounds
Knit 2 rounds in CC
Purl 2 rounds in MC
BO purlwise in MC.

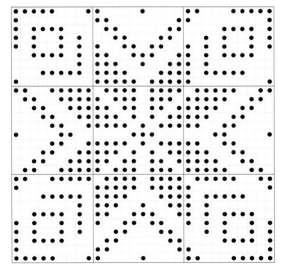

☐ MC (Main Colour)   ● CC (Contrast Colour)

MAKING UP

Darn in all ends. Press on wrong side of work. Stretch elastic around intended wearer's waist – cut to fit plus an extra 5 cm (2 in) for overlap. With skirt inside out lay elastic out on wrong side of front facing section of waistband. Pin in place, ensuring all pins are inserted from the right side of the skirt. Overlap elastic by 2.5 cm (1 in) and sew the two ends securely together, taking care not to attach to skirt. Fold upper half of waistband to inside of skirt along fold line (purl row) and slip stitch into place. Now remove pins holding elastic in place. (Can only be done if pins are on right side of waistband!). If preferred, to prevent movement or curling of elastic, sew through both layers of waistband and elastic at skirt sides using matching thread. This will allow the elastic to continue to stretch within each half of the skirt but will stop the elastic twisting within the waistband.

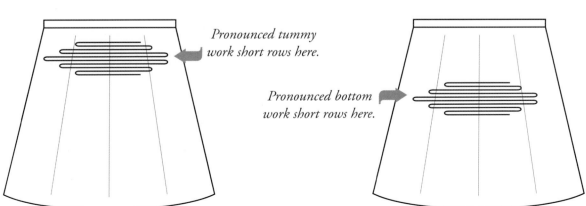

FITTING TIPS

If the intended wearer has either a rounded tummy or a pronounced bottom, work some short rows as suggested in the diagrams below.

Pronounced tummy work short rows here.

Pronounced bottom work short rows here.

This delightful jacket is the perfect cover up over a summer dress
or an extra layer in the cooler months.

Adorable Little Bed Jacket with Hood

This delicious little bed jacket is knitted in a sweet lacy pattern and is completed with a dramatic opera cloak style hood, to frame the face. Flattering three quarter length sleeves, edge to edge finishing and a stylish ribbon to draw the jacket closed finish off this most elegant of jackets.

MATERIALS
Rowan Pure Wool 4 ply (fingering weight) (approx160 m /176 yds per 50 gm ball)
7 (8, 9, 10, 11, 12) balls shade 449 (vintage)
3.25 mm (US 4) needles
2 m (or 2 yds) contrasting Ribbon

TENSION
Standard yarn tension: 28 sts & 36 rows = 10 cm (4 inches) using 3.25 mm (US 4) needles over stocking stitch.
Pattern tension: 3 pattern repeats using 3.25 mm (US 4) needles = 6.5 cm (2.5 inches)

PATTERN NOTES
The 4 row pattern used for this garment looses stitches on row 1 which are replaced on row 2. It is therefore unadvisable to do stitch counts after row 1. The stitch pattern is worked over 6 sts + 7. Please note the pattern spreads significantly on blocking and it is important to block your tension square to compare your tension to the pattern.

BACK
CO 127 (139, 151, 163, 175, 187) sts using 3.25 mm (US 4) needles.
Row 1 (RS): P2, * yb, sl1, K2tog, psso, P3 * rep from * to end, finishing last rep with P2.
Row 2: K2, *yrn, P1, yrn, K3 * rep from * to end, finishing last rep with K2.

To Fit (after blocking)						
in	30–34	36–38	40–42	44–46	48–50	52–54
cm	76–86	91–96	101–107	112–117	122–127	132–137
Actual Size						
in	33	37	41	45	49	53
cm	84	94	104	114	124.5	134.5
Length to underarm						
in	12.5	13	13.5	14.5	15	16
cm	32	33	34	37	38	40.5
Finished Length						
in	18.5	20	20.5	22.5	23.5	25
cm	47	51	52	57	60	63.5
Sleeve Length						
in	11	11	11	11	12	12
cm	28	28	28	28	30.5	30.5

Our model is photographed wearing 76–86 cm (30–34 inch) jacket

Row 3: P2, *K3, P3, rep from * to end, finishing last rep with P2.
Row 4: K2, *P3, K3, rep from * to end, finishing last rep with K2.
These 4 rows complete the pattern.

Continue as set working these 4 pattern rows until work measures 30.5 (32, 33, 35.5, 37, 39) cm (12, 12.5, 13, 14, 14.5, 15.5 inches) ending with row 2.

ARMHOLE SHAPING
Keeping the 4 row pattern throughout work decreases as folls:
Rows 1 and 2: BO 7 sts at beg of row.
Row 3: BO 3 sts at beg of row.
Row 4: BO 3 sts at beg of row.
Row 5: Work 2 sts tog at beg and end of every row until 101 (109, 117, 125, 133, 141) sts remain. Continue without further shaping until armhole measures approx 15.25 (18, 18, 20, 21.5, 23) cm (6, 7, 7, 8, 8.5, 9 inches) ending with row 2.

SHOULDER SHAPING
BO 11 (11, 12, 13, 14, 15) sts at beg of next 6 rows.
Next row: BO remaining 35 (43, 45, 47, 49, 51) sts.

RIGHT FRONT
CO 67 (73, 79, 85, 91, 97) sts using 3.25 mm (US 4) needles.
Working 4 row pattern as for back, continue until work measures 30.5 (32, 33, 35.5, 37, 39) cm (12, 12.5, 13, 14, 14.5, 15.5 inches).

ARMHOLE SHAPING
Row 1: BO 7 sts, pattern to end.
Row 2: Patt to end.
Row 3: BO 3 sts, pattern to end.
Row 4: Pattern to last 2 stitches, work 2 sts tog.
Row 5: K2tog, patt to end.
Row 6: Pattern to last 2 stitches work 2 sts tog.
Rep rows 5 and 6 until 54 (54, 57, 60, 63, 66 sts) rem. Continue without shaping, until armhole measures approx 14 (16.5, 16.5, 19, 20, 21.5) cm (5.5, 6.5, 6.5, 7.5, 8, 8.5 inches).

NECK SHAPING
Row 1: BO 13 sts at neck edge, pattern to end.
Row 2: Patt to end.
Row 3 and foll 3 alt rows: Work 2 sts tog, patt to end.
Row 4 and foll 2 RS rows: Patt to last 2 sts, work 2 sts tog (34, 34, 37, 40, 43, 46 sts).

NECK SHAPING

Row 1: BO 13 sts at neck edge, pattern to end.

Row 2: Patt to end.

Row 3 and foll 3 alt rows: Work 2 sts tog, patt to end.

Row 4 and foll 2 RS rows: Patt to last 2 sts, work 2 sts tog (34, 34, 37, 40, 43, 46 sts).

SHOULDER SHAPING:

Row 1: BO 11 (11, 12, 13, 14, 15) sts, patt to end.

Row 2: Patt to end.

Row 3: BO 11 (11, 12, 13, 14, 15) sts, patt to end.

Row 4: Patt to end.

Next row: BO remaining sts.

SLEEVES (MAKE TWO)

CO 103 (109, 115, 121, 127, 133) sts using 3.25 mm (US 4) needles.

Commencing with row 1 of 4 row pattern, continue until work measures approx 28 cm 28 (28, 28, 28, 30.5, 30.5) cm (11, 11, 11, 11, 12, 12 inches).

SHOULDER SHAPING

Row 1: BO 11 (11, 12, 13, 14, 15) sts, patt to end.

Row 2: Patt to end.

Row 3: BO 11 (11, 12, 13, 14, 15) sts, patt to end.

Row 4: Patt to end.

Next row: BO remaining sts.

LEFT FRONT

Work as Right Front until work measures 30.5 (32, 33, 35.5, 37, 39) cm (12, 12.5, 13, 14, 14.5, 15.5 inches).

Row 1: BO 7 sts, work to end.

Row 2: Patt to end.

Row 3: BO 3 sts, patt to end.

Row 4: Patt to last 2 sts, work 2 sts tog.

Row 5: Work 2 sts tog, patt to end.

Row 6: Patt to last 2 sts, work 2 sts tog. Rep rows 5 and 6 until 54 (54, 57, 60, 63, 66 sts) rem. Continue without shaping, until armhole measures approx 14 (16.5, 16.5, 19, 20, 21.5) cm (5.5, 6.5, 6.5, 7.5, 8, 8.5 inches).

This simple lace stitch is a great introduction to lace knitting.

SHAPE TOP

Row 1: BO 6 sts, patt to end.

Row 2: BO 6 sts, pattern to end (91, 97, 103, 109, 115, 121 sts).

Row 3: Work 2 tog, patt to end.

Continue working as for row 3 until 57 (57, 63, 63, 69, 69) sts rem.

Next row: BO remaining sts.

HOOD

CO 97 sts using 3.25 mm (US 4) needles.

Commencing with row 1 of 4 row pattern, continue until work measures 30.5 (32, 33, 34, 35.5, 37) cm (12, 12.5, 13, 13.5, 14, 14.5 inches) ending with row 4.

Next row: BO 13 sts.

Work in pattern for 10 cm (4 inches).

Next row: CO 13 sts.

Continue in pattern until hood measures 71 (74, 76, 78, 81, 84) cm (28, 29, 30, 31, 32, 33 inches) from beginning of work.

Next row: BO all sts.

MAKING UP

With work RS down, pin out pieces and block well. The pattern spreads significantly on pressing. Darn in all ends. Join shoulder seams. To join hood, fold 13 extra sts in and stitch to straight edge, creating horizontal seam at top back of hood. Stitch together back seam. Starting at left front pin hood to jacket body with RS together as far as shoulder seams, leaving approx 2 cm (three quarters of an inch) extended at end beyond front edge. Pin for approx 5 cm (2 inches) beyond shoulder seam then work right side of hood and jacket to match. At this point gather remaining hood seam together easing work to fit to centre back seam (see photo). This creates a very gathered up area at the back of the hood. Sew together. Fold edge of hood inwards, pinning in place along length of hood front. Fold ribbon in half and match centre of ribbon with centre front of hood. Pin in place to approx 2.5 cm (1 inch) beyond hood onto front of jacket encasing folded edge of hood underneath. Slip stitch into place along both edges of ribbon, securing hood edge.

Insert sleeves by pinning armhole cast off edges together and matching centre sleeve head with shoulder seam. Work without gathering until centre top 7.5 cm (3 inches). At this point gather top of sleeve head to fit into remaining armhole. Sew up side and sleeve seams.

Sugar and Spice and all things nice, thats what these gifts are made of!

Sugar and Spice

These pretty, vintage influenced dressing gowns make great gifts

MATERIALS

Rowan Handknit DK cotton (100% machine washable cotton) – This is a slightly thick DK (8 ply) weight yarn
11 (12) balls x shade 239 (ice water)
or shade 332 (rose)

1 pair 3.25 mm (US 4) needles
1 pair 3.75 mm (US 5) needles
1 pair 4 mm (US 6) needles
1 cable needle (optional)
6 Buttons

This yarn has been chosen as it can be both machine washed and tumble dried if required, which for a toddlers dressing gown seems a more than sensible precaution!

Designed to reach the floor when worn, these dressing gowns can easily be shortened or lengthened. They can also be worn long after they no longer reach the floor affording a long life to these beautiful garments.

To fit		
Age	1 – 2 yrs	2 – 3 yrs
Height	2 ft 6 in – 3 ft 80 – 92 cm	3 ft – 3 ft 3 in 92 – 98 cm
Chest	20 – 21 in 51 – 53.5 cm	21 – 22 in 53.5 – 56 cm
Actual Chest Size	30 in 76 cm	30 in 76 cm
Finished Length	26 in 66 cm	27 in 68.5 cm
Sleeve Length	6.5 in 16.5 cm	7.5 in 19 cm

TENSION

20 sts and 26 rows to 10 cm (4 inches) using 4 mm (US 6) needles over stocking stitch.

PATTERN NOTES

Edging Pattern

Row 1: *T2f, T2b, rep from * to end
Row 2: Purl
Row 3: *T2b, T2f, rep from * to end
Row 4: Purl

T2f & T2b can be worked with or without a cable needle as follows:

Wrap in tissue and tie a matching ribbon around to make a beautiful christening gift.

Without a cable needle

T2f – purl into back of 2nd st on left needle, then knit 1st st slipping both sts off needle at the same time.

T2b – Knit into front of 2nd st on left needle then purl first st slipping both sts off needle at the same time.

With a cable needle

T2f – Slip next st onto cable needle and hold at front of work, purl next st on left needle then knit st from cable needle.

T2b – Slip next st onto cable needle and hold at back of work, knit next st from left needle then purl st from cable needle.

*Why not knit a red dressing gown
for a festive christmas present?*

BACK

CO 112 sts using 3.75 mm (US 5) needles and work 5 rows in garter st.

Next row: Purl.

Commence patt as folls:

Row 1 (RS): *T2f, T2b, rep from * to end.

Row 2: Purl.

Row 3: *T2b, T2f, rep from * to end.

Row 4: Purl.

Rep these 4 rows of patt twice more then 1st row only, once more.

Next row: p4, *P2tog, P2 rep from * to last 4 sts, P4 (86 sts).

Change to 4 mm (US 6) needles and beg with a K row, work in st st, dec 1 st at each end of 20th row and every foll 21st row until 74 sts rem. Continue without further shaping until back measures 52 (54) cm (20.5, 21 inches), or desired length, from cast on edge ending with a P row.

Shape raglans

** BO 4 sts at beg of next 2 rows.

Next row: K1, SL1, K1, psso, K to last 3 sts, K2tog, K1.

Next row: Purl.

Rep last 2 rows **** until 30 sts rem.

Next row: K1, SL1, K1, psso, K to last 3 sts, K2tog, K1.

Next row: P1, P2tog, P to last 3 sts, P2togtbl, P1.

Rep last 2 rows until 18 sts rem.

BO all rem sts.

LEFT FRONT

CO 52 sts using 3.75 mm (US 5) needles and commence edging pattern as given for back.

Next row: Purl, decreasing 10 sts evenly across row (42 sts).

Change to 4mm (US 6) needles and work in st st, dec 1 st at side edge of 20th row and every foll 21st row until 36 sts rem.

Continue without further shaping until front measures same as back to start of raglan shaping.

Shape raglans

BO 4 sts at beg of next row.

Work 1 row.

Next row: K1, SL1, K1, psso, K to end.

Next row: Purl.

Rep last 2 rows until 16 sts remain, ending at neck edge.

BO 2 sts at beg of next row.

Next row: K1, SL1, K1, psso, K to last 2 sts, K2tog.

Next row: P2tog, P to last 3 sts, P2togtbl, P1.

Rep last 2 rows until 2 sts rem.

K2tog, fasten off.

RIGHT FRONT

Work as left front reversing all shapings.

SLEEVES

Cast on 52 sts using 3.75 mm (US 5) needles and work 5 rows in garter st.
Next row: Purl.
Work edging patt as given for back.
Next row: P, dec 12 sts evenly across row (40 sts).

Work 9 rows in K1, P1 rib.

Change to 4 mm (US 6) needles and beg with a knit row, work in st st, inc 1st at each end of 4th and every foll 3rd (4th) row until there are 62 sts on needle. Continue without further shaping until sleeve measures 16.5 (19) cm (6.5, 7.5 inches) from beg of rib ending with a P row.

Shape raglans

Follow instructions as given for back from ** to *** until 20 sts rem. Then dec 1st at each end of every row until 6 sts rem. BO all rem sts.

COLLAR

CO 64 sts using 3.75 mm (US 5) needles and work 5 rows in garter st.
Next row: K2, P to last 2 sts, K2.

Keeping 2 sts at each end of row in garter st., repeat 4 row edging patt as given for back 4 times.

Shape collar

Row 1: K2, patt to last 12 sts, turn.
Row 2: P to last 12 sts. turn.
Row 3: Patt to last 24 sts, turn.
Row 4: P to last 24 sts, turn.

Cut yarn, slip all sts onto one needle. Rejoin yarn to end of row and working across all sts, bind off.

MAKING UP

Darn in all ends. Join raglans.

Using 3.25 mm (US 4) needles, and with RS facing, pick up 146 (152) sts down left front.
Work 6 rows in K2, P2 rib. BO fairly loosely in rib.

Using 3.25 mm (US 4) needles, and with RS facing, pick up 146 (152) sts up right front.
Work 2 rows in K2, P2 rib.
Next row: Patt 2 sts, (BO next 2 sts, patt 14 sts) 5 times, BO next 2 sts, patt to end.
Next row: (Patt to bound off sts., turn work, CO 2 sts, bringing yarn fwd between the 2 cast on sts before placing 2nd st onto left hand needle, turn) 6 times. Patt 2 sts.

Work 2 rows in rib pattern as set. BO fairly loosely in rib.

Sew up side and sleeve seams, using flat seam on cuffs. Attach collar using edge to edge flat seam, positioning collar at points where rib meets fronts and centre of collar to centre back. Sew on buttons in line with buttonholes. Fold cuffs back as shown. Catch stitch in place.

Not just for fathers, but great for husbands, boy friends, brothers and cousins.

Father's New Socks

Made using a standard 4 ply yarn and only needing 50 gms of each colour it is also a great stash busting project.

These fabulous socks are far simpler than they look, using an easy 2 colour slip stitch pattern to create a 'fair isle' style pattern. These socks are worked from the top down and can therefore be made to whatever leg length required. Instructions are also given in the 'To Fit' section explaining how to alter sock foot length.

MATERIALS
Jamieson & Smith 2 Ply Jumper Weight Yarn (100% shetland wool) – knits up as a 4 ply (fingering weight) yarn (115m / 125 yds per 25 gm ball)
Main Colour – shade FC64 – 2 balls (MC)
Contrast Colour – shade 1A – 2 balls (CC)
Set of 2.75 mm (US 2) dpns
Set of 3.25 mm (US 4) dpns

TENSION
30 sts & 40 rows over slip stitch pattern using 3.25 mm (US 4) dpns and 2 yarns

The pattern is written for a men's UK size 11 foot (US 11.5, Euro 45). To adjust the foot length simply reduce or increase the length worked at this point *** bearing in mind the toe measures an additional 5.75 cm (2.25 inches). Therefore as in this example if the foot measures 28 cm (11 inches) from heel to toe, work sole of heel until measures 8.75 inches from base of heel, leaving 2.25 inches for toe to be worked (total length 8.75 + 2.25 = 11 inches).

Sock circumference 25.5 cm (10 inches) Leg length (to top of heel) also 25.5 cm (10 inches)

PATTERN

CO 72 sts, using MC and 2.75 mm (US 2) dpns, placing 24 sts onto each of 3 needles. Join into a round placing a marker at the beginning of the round.
First round: K1, P1, to end. Repeat this round until work measures 9 cm (3.5 inches).
Change to 3.25 mm (US 4) dpns and work pattern as folls:
Round 1: Using CC, K.
Round 2: Using MC, * SL1, K3, rep from * to end of round.
Round 3: as round 2.
Round 4: as round 1.
Round 5: Using MC, *SL1, K5, rep from * to end of round.
Round 6: as round 5.
These 6 rounds form pattern.

Continue in pattern until work measures 25.5 cm (10 inches) from cast on edge, or desired length, ending with round 6.

DIVIDE FOR THE HEEL

Slip 18 sts from first needle and same from third needle onto one needle (36 sts for heel). Divide the remaining 36 sts onto 2 needles to work instep.

HEEL

Change to 2.75 mm (US 2) dpns and rejoin MC to beg of heel sts with WS facing.
Row 1: P.
Row 2: * SL1, K1, rep from * to end.
Rep these 2 rows until heel measures 5.75 cm (2.25 inches). Work row 1 once more.

TO TURN HEEL

Row 1: K21, K2tog, K1, turn.
Row 2: SL1, P7, P2tog, P1, turn.
Row 3: SL1, K8, K2tog, K1, turn.
Row 4: SL1, P9, P2tog, P1, turn.
Row 5: SL1, K10, K2tog, K1, turn.
Row 6: SL1, P11, P2tog, P1, turn.

Continue in this manner increasing the number of stitches worked before working 2 sts tog on each subsequent row, until 14 rows worked in total.
Next row (row 15): K22, pick up and knit 15 sts down side of heel, turn, P37, pick up and purl 15 sts down other side of heel, turn (52 sts).

SHAPE INSTEP

Row 1: K1, SL1, K1, psso, knit to last 3 sts, K2tog, K1.
Row 2: P.
Repeat these 2 rows until 34 sts remain.
Work without shaping on these 34 sts until foot measures 22 cm (8.75 inches) or required length ***.
Leave sts on spare needle.

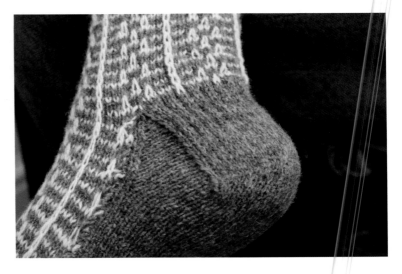

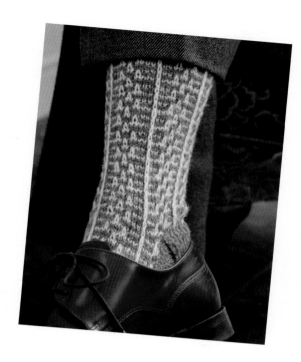

SHAPE TOE

Divide sts over three 3.25 mm (US 4) dpns as follows: 34 sts PM, 17 sts, 17sts PM. Using 4th dpn and MC only work as folls:

Round 1: K1, SL1, K1, psso, K to last 3 sts before first marker, K2tog, K1, SM, K1, SL1, K1, psso, K to last 3 sts before second marker, K2tog, K1, SM.
Round 2: K.

Rep these 2 rounds until 28 sts rem in total. Divide these sts equally onto 2 dpns with last st worked at right hand end of needle to commence grafting. Cut yarn long enough to graft the 14 sts together and thread onto sewing up needle. Graft sts together.

Darn in all ends.

Change to 3.25 mm (US 4) dpns and join CC to instep sts. K one row, picking up 1 st at each end of row from edge of sole and knitting it together with first and last st of pattern row. Join in MC and beginning with row 2 of pattern, work 3 rows of pattern, at the end of each picking up and knitting 1 st tog with first and last sts of pattern row. Join in a 2nd ball of MC and work rows 5 and 6 of patt, picking up sts as before. Continue in this manner using separate balls of MC for rows 2 and 3 then 5 and 6 and always picking up a st as described, until instep measures the same as sole, ending with 1st or 4th row. Work one purl row in MC.

What little girl doesn't like bunnies?

Hearts and Bunnies Cardigan

This cute little cardigan was inspired by Anouk in the film Chocolat and knitwear worn by children in the 1940s but with a more contemporary colour scheme to appeal to today's little girls. Another great stash busting project as nearly all of the colours use less than 1 50 gm ball of wool. The pretty buttons are also knitted, take very little time to make and use hardly any yarn – another tip from the 1940s!

MATERIALS

Biggan Design 4 ply Merino First Cross
100% merino wool (180 m/196 yds per 50gm ball)
Main Colour (MC) – shade 925 (rose) – 3 balls
(A) – shade 610 (spruce) – 1 ball
(B) – shade 080 (white) – 1 ball
(C) – shade 915 (vintage rose) – 1 ball

Rowan pure wool 4 ply (100% wool)
(160 m/174 yds per 50 gm ball)
(D) – shade 450 (eau de nil) – 2 balls.
(E) – shade 417 (mocha) – 1 ball
These are standard 4 ply (fingering weight) yarns

1 pair 3 mm (US 3) needles
1 pair 3.25 mm (US 4) needles

TO FIT			
Ages	1-2	2-3	3-4
Chest			
in	20-21	21-22	22-24
cm	51-53.5	53.5-56	56-61
Actual Chest Size			
in	24	26	28
cm	61	66	71
Length to underarm			
in	10.5	11	11.5
cm	26.5	28	29
Finished length			
in	15.5	16	17.5
cm	39	40.5	44.5
Sleeve length			
in	8	9	10
cm	20	23	25.5

PATTERN NOTES

This cardigan is knitted in one piece from the welt to the underarm, where it is then divided and worked in separate pieces. Chart A is knitted by carrying (stranding) the yarns across the back of the work using Fair Isle techniques – resulting in a double layer of fabric, and Chart B is worked in intarsia, using separate small balls of each colour for each area of the pattern. The colours are not carried across the work creating a single layer of fabric.

PATTERN

CO 162 (174, 186) sts using 3.25 mm (US 4) needles in MC.

Next row: *K1, P1, rep from * to end.

Rep this row a further 11(15, 19) times, inc 6 sts evenly across last row (168, 180, 192 sts).

Commencing with a K row now work in st st throughout.

Work 2 rows.

Now commencing with row 1, work the 22 rows of chart A, using fair isle technique.

Next row (RS): Commencing with row 1 work the 34 rows of Chart B using intarsia technique and separate small balls of yarn for each section.

Commencing with row 1, work the 22 rows of chart A once again.

DIVIDE FOR ARMHOLES

Change to shade A, K37 (40, 43), BO 9, K76 (82, 88), BO 9, K37 (40, 43) .

Work on these last 37 (40, 43) sts only.

Next row: P to end.

Next and every foll K row: K1, SL1, K1, psso, K to end.

Repeat these 2 rows until 25 (25, 28) sts rem, ending with a RS row.

NECK SHAPING

Next row (WS): BO 2, P to end.

Next row: K1 SL1, psso, K to end.

Repeat these 2 rows twice more (16, 16, 19 sts).

Next row: P.

Next row: K1, SL1, psso, K to last 2 sts, K2tog.

Rep these 2 rows until 6 sts rem ending with a WS row.

Continue decreasing at armhole edge on RS row only, three more times (3 sts).

Next row: P.

Next row: K3tog, draw yarn through and fasten off.

With WS of work facing, rejoin yarn to 76 (82, 88) sts for back, and P to end.

Next row: K1, SL1, psso, patt to last 3 sts, K2tog, K1.

Next row: P.

Rep these last 2 rows until 30 sts rem, ending with a WS row. Leave rem sts on holder.

With WS of work facing, rejoin yarn to rem 37 (40, 43) sts and work as for left front but reversing all shapings.

SLEEVES

CO 42 (48, 54) sts using 3 mm (US 3) needles and MC. Work 12 (16, 20) rows of K1, P1, rib.

Change to 3.25 mm (US 4) needles and work in stocking stitch, increasing 1 st at each end of 3rd and every foll 2nd (2nd, 3rd) row until 66 (72, 78) sts.

Continue without shaping until sleeves measures 20 (23, 25.5) cm (8, 9, 10 inches) ending with a WS row.

RAGLAN SHAPING

BO 4 sts at beg of next 2 rows.

Next row: K1, SL1, K1, psso, patt to last 3 sts, K2tog, K1.

Next row: Purl.

Repeat these 2 rows until 6 sts rem. Leave these sts on holder.

BANDS

Join raglan seams using a neat backstitch.

Right front band

Using 3 mm (US 3) needles and with RS of work facing, pick up and K 104 (112, 120) sts up right front.

Next row (WS): * P2, K2, rep from * to end.

Next row (RS): * P2, K2, rep from * to end.

Rep these 2 rows once more, then first row one more time.

Knitted buttons save money and always match exactly!

Next row (buttonhole row): Patt 4, ** BO foll 1 st, patt 7, rep from ** 11(12, 13) times, BO foll 1 st, patt to end.

Next row: *** Patt to BO st, turn, Co 1, turn, rep from *** to last 4 sts, patt to end.

Work 5 more rows in rib patt, then BO in rib.

Left front band

Using 3 mm (US 3) needles and with RS of work facing, pick up and K 104 (112, 120) sts down left front.

Next row (WS): * K2, P2, rep from * to end.

Next row (RS): * K2, P2, rep from * to end.

Rep these 2 rows 5 times more (12 rows worked in total).

BO in rib.

NECKBAND

Using 3 mm (US 3) needles, and with RS of work facing, pick up 10 sts across right front band, 16 (18, 20) sts up right side neck, K 6 sts from sleeve, 30 sts across back, 6 sts from 2nd sleeve, 16 (18, 20) sts down left front side and 10 sts across left band (94, 98, 102 sts).

Next row (WS): * P2, K2, rep from * to last 2 sts, P2.

Next row: * K2, P2, rep from * to last 2 sts, K2.

Repeat first row once more.

Next row (buttonhole row): Patt 4, BO foll 1 st, patt to end.

Next row: Patt to BO st, turn, CO 1 st, turn, patt 4 sts.

Work 3 more rows in rib patt, then BO in rib.

MAKING UP

Darn in all ends. Sew up side and sleeve seams using a neat back stitch.

Chart A

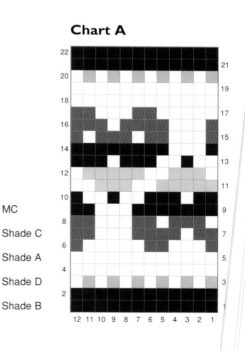

MC
Shade C
Shade A
Shade D
Shade B

*Great for using up
left over balls of wool.*

TO MAKE BUTTONS

CO 6 sts using 3 mm (US 3) needles, commencing with a K row, work in st st for 6 rows. BO. Cut yarn, leaving a length approx 20 cm (8 inches) long attached to knitting. Thread sewing up needle and work running stitch around the edges of the knitted square. Once you have gone right round the square, draw in sts. Before closing up completely, use tail remaining from slip knot cast on as stuffing. Push inside button and draw up completely. Sew up firmly then use same length of yarn to sew button into place on button band.

Repeat a further 13 (14, 15) times.

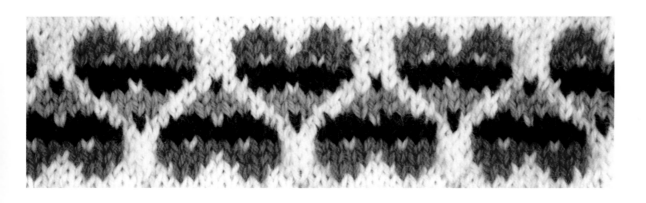

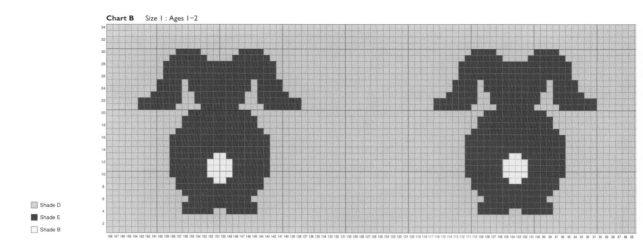

Shade D
Shade E
Shade B

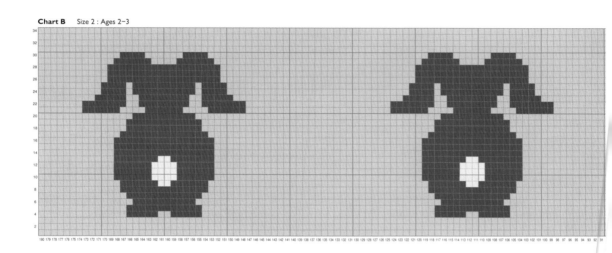

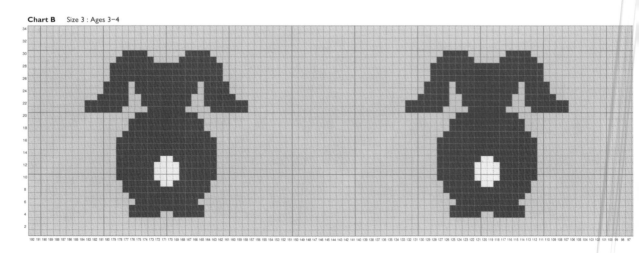

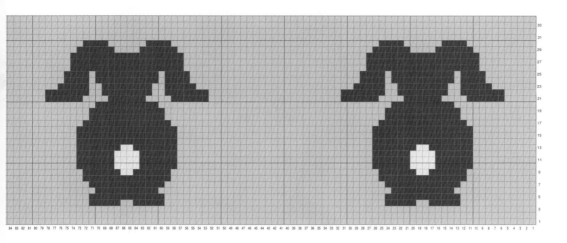

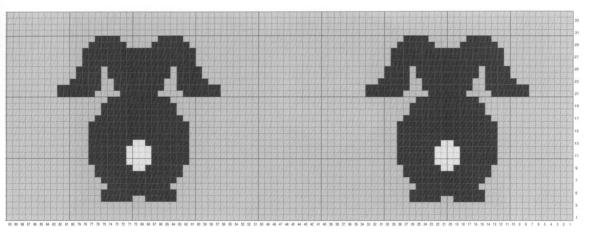

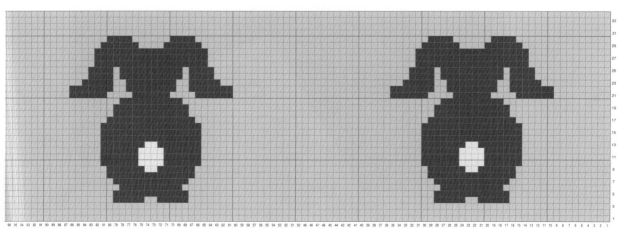

Our model, Miss Moon always ensures she has a coordinating corsage pinned to her lapel.

A Simply Perfect Corsage

This incredibly simply pattern provides the starting blocks to all manner of beautiful corsages, brooches and hair decorations. The pattern illustrates two distinctly different finished pieces from the same pattern, both taking around an hour to make and using only a few grams of yarn.

The two projects shown use different weight yarns but the same needle size. The pattern can be followed using thicker or thinner yarn, smaller or bigger needles, all just resulting in bigger or smaller finished items. Decorate with oddments of ribbon, lace, buttons and beads for a truly vintage looking piece.

MATERIALS

Oddments of 4 ply (fingering weight) yarn
1 pair 3.25 mm (US 4) needles
Sewing up needle
Notions to embellish – buttons, ribbon, lace, beads etc
Sewing up thread
Brooch fastening, dress clip fastening, hair slide or simply a safety pin
Small piece of fabric

TENSION

Tension is not important for this pattern. Adjust depending on how you want the finished piece to hang.

FLOWER CORSAGE

Make 4 petals as above. Press. Pin the 4 petals in a circle – with bound off edge facing inwards (I pin them onto the back of a cushion). Slip stitch the petals together along the diagonal edges for about 2.5 cm (1 inch) using yarn remaining from bound off sts. Darn in other ends.

Thread sewing up needle with length of yarn and work running sts around inner edge were the petals meet. Take care just to take the needle between the sts rather than breaking through the sts themselves. Once you are back at the beginning draw the sts together by pulling both ends. Pull until all sts are pulled tightly together and there are no gaps. Take needle through centre of sts to back of work, pull tighter again and then sew into place. Darn in rem ends. Fill centre of flower with decorative button. From back of corsage sew coordinating ribbon as shown.

Cut small circular piece of coordinating fabric – felt is good if you have it, as it doesn't need hemming. If necessary, hem and slip stitch into place over centre back of corsage. Attach brooch clip or safety pin to the back of the corsage. Alternatively, this corsage could be attached to a hair slide for a pretty hair piece or attached to a firm piece of ribbon and tied at the wrist or round the neck.

BASIC PETAL PATTERN

CO 8 sts using 3.25 mm (US 4) needles.
Row 1 and foll WS rows (WS): P.
Next and foll 4 RS rows: K1, M1, K to last st, M1, K1 (18 sts).
Once 18 sts on needle work 3 rows in st st.
Dec 1 st at each end of next 5 rows until 8 sts rem, ending with WS facing.
BO all sts knitwise leaving a long thread.

BEADED BOW DRESS CLIPS (make two)

Dress clips were frequently worn as dress decoration during the first half of the twentieth century. Originals are getting harder to find, but can still be spotted in second hand and charity shops, sometimes wrongly identified as a brooch. Single or damaged dress clips can be picked up very cheaply and the clip part re-used as a fastening as suggested here.

MATERIALS

Oddment of Tilli Thomas Rock Star Rattan 100% silk with glass beads (alternatively thread some beads onto the yarn of your choice and knit in randomly)

1 pair 3.25 mm (US 4) needles

Make as gifts or knit to complement your own wardrobe.

C O 8 sts using 3.25 mm (US 4) needles. Work in garter stitch throughout.

Row 1 and foll WS rows (WS): K.

Next and foll 4 RS rows: K1, M1, K to last st, M1, K1 (18 sts).

Once 18 sts on needle work 3 rows in garter st.

Dec 1 st at each end of next 5 rows until 8 sts rem, ending with WS facing.

Work two more rows without shaping.

Next and foll 4 rows: Inc 1 at each end of row (18 sts).

Work 3 rows without shaping.

Dec 1 st at each end of next and foll 4 alt rows until 8 sts rem.

Knit 1 row.

BO knitwise.

D arn in all ends. Take length of yarn and starting at centre back of bow, wrap yarn around the centre, pulling the work in closer together and emphasising the bow shape. Tie in knot at back of work then darn in ends. Sew dress clips to back. Alternatively add fastening as for Flower Corsage.

Wear at neckline, clipped to collars or even together to one side of garment, for a 1930s asymmetric look.

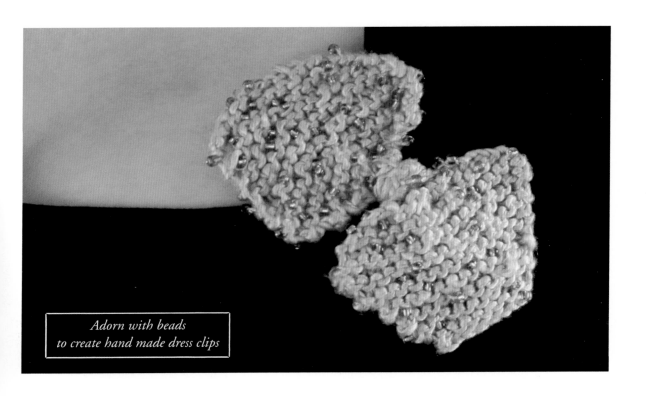

*Adorn with beads
to create hand made dress clips*

A well dressed lady is never seen out without her gloves!

Gloves for a Spring Wedding

These dainty gloves are just the thing for a spring or summer wedding. Knitted in a standard 4 ply yarn and taking less than 100 gm to make a pair, these gloves also make excellent presents. Try knitting them in white cotton for a high summer effect or in colours to complement your entire wardrobe!

MATERIALS

Skein Queen Blush (80% merino, 20% cashmere) 4 ply yarn (397 m/435 yds per 100 gm skein) – This is a 4 ply (fingering weight) yarn.
1 skein – shade Kite Flying
1 pair 2.25 mm (US 1) needles
Set of 5 2.5 mm (US 2) dpns
2 stitch markers
4 small buttons

TENSION

30 sts & 40 rows = 10 cm (4 inches) over stocking stitch using 2.5 mm (US 2) needles

RIGHT GLOVE

Cast on 55 (65) sts using 2.25 mm (US 1) straight needles.

Row 1 (RS): K1, *P1, K1, rep from * to end.

Row 2: as row 1.

Row 3 (buttonhole row): K1, P1, BO 1, patt to end.

Row 4: Patt to BO stitch, turn work, cast on 1 st using cable cast on, bringing yarn forward between sts before placing CO st onto LH needle, turn again, patt to end.

Work 4 rows as row 1.

Repeat rows 3 and 4 once more.

Work 2 rows as row 1.

Change to 2.5 mm (US 2) needles and commencing with a K row, work 4 rows in st st.

Row 1 (RS): K22 (27), YO, SL1, K2tog, psso, YO, K9, YO, SL1, K2tog, psso, YO* K18 (23).

Row 2 and all even rows: Purl.

Row 3: K17 (22), (YO, K2tog, K1, K2tog, YO, K3, YO, K2tog, K2) twice, K14 (19).

SHAPE THUMB

Row 5: as row 1 to * PM, Kfb, K4, Kfb, PM, K12 (17).

Row 7: K16 (21), YO, SL1, K2tog, psso, YO, K9, YO, SL1, K2tog, psso, YO, K26 (31).

Row 9: K14 (19), *K2tog, YO, K3, YO, K2tog, K2, YO, K2tog** K1, rep from * to ** once, SM, Kfb, K6, Kfb, K12 (17).

Row 11: as row 7, but please note, number of sts to be knit at end of row will now alter due to increases being worked at thumb.

Row 12: as row 2.

These 12 rows complete pattern.

Next row: as row 1 to *, SM, Kfb, K8, Kfb, SM, K12 (14).

Next row: as row 2.

Join into rounds, dividing sts between 3 dpns, placing last 5 sts behind first 5 sts, knit them together then continue as for row 3.

Continue working in rounds, knitting every other round, and increasing 2 sts for thumb gusset on row 5 and every foll 4th row 4 times (22 sts between markers).

Next round: Patt to first marker, slip next 22 sts onto waste yarn, CO 2, K7 (12).
Work in pattern without shaping until row 12 completed, or hand of glove is required length (always ending with an even row).

FIRST FINGER

K30 (35), leave these sts on waste yarn, K14 (16), place rem 1 (5) sts on waste yarn. CO 4 sts for the inside of the finger and work in rounds on these 18 (20) sts only until finger is required length.

TO SHAPE TOP

Next round: (K2tog, K1) to last 2 sts, K2tog.
Next round: K2tog to end. Draw thread through rem sts and fasten off on inside of finger.

SECOND & THIRD FINGERS

K6 (7) sts off front of glove, pick up and knit 5 sts from bottom of first finger, K5 (6) (16, 18 sts).

SECOND SIZE ONLY

Next round: K8, (K2tog) twice, K6 (16 sts).

BOTH SIZES

Work as for first finger until required length.

TO SHAPE TOP

Next round: K1 (K2tog, K1) to end.
Next round: K2tog to end. Draw thread through rem sts and fasten off on inside of finger.

FOURTH FINGER

Knit rem 10 (14) sts, pick up and knit 4 sts across bottom of third finger (14, 18 sts).

SECOND SIZE ONLY
Next round: K7, (K2tog) twice, K7 (16 sts).

BOTH SIZES
Work until required length.

Shape top as for second finger.

THUMB
K22 sts from waste yarn then pick up 7 sts across bottom of first finger (29 sts)
Next round: K21, (K2tog) 4 times (25 sts).
Next round: K17, (K2tog) 4 times (21 sts).
Work until required length.

TO SHAPE TOP
Next round: (K2tog, K1) to end.
Next round: K2tog to end. Draw thread through rem sts and fasten off on inside of thumb.

LEFT GLOVE
Work as for right glove but work buttonholes at the end of rows 3 and 9.
Continue as for right glove until thumb placement.
Work as follows:

Row 5: K12 (17) PM, Kfb, K4, Kfb, PM, K4 *YO, SL1, K2tog, psso, YO, K9, rep from * once more, K to end.

Continue as for right glove, working lace pattern to fit new position, remembering that the number of stitches worked at beginning of round will alter.

Work 1 row. Join into round as for right glove but place last 5 sts in FRONT of first 5 sts and then knit together. Continue until hand is same length as right glove to start of finger placement.

FIRST FINGER PLACEMENT
K to within 7 (8) sts of first marker, SM, K14 (16), place all remaining sts other than 14 (16) just knitted onto waste yarn. CO 4 sts across finger space (18, 20 sts).

With first finger in position work each finger as for right glove.

MAKING UP
Darn in all remaining ends. Sew buttons in place opposite buttonholes. If necessary, place damp cloth over gloves and press lightly with a steam iron.

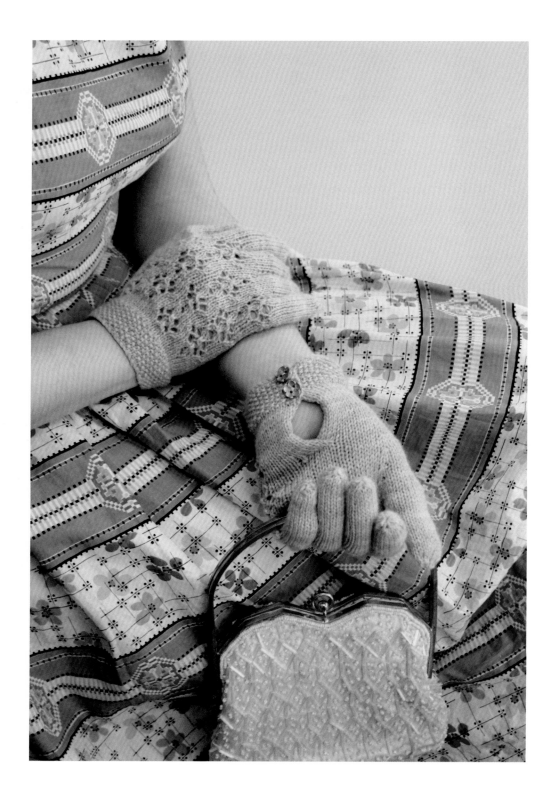

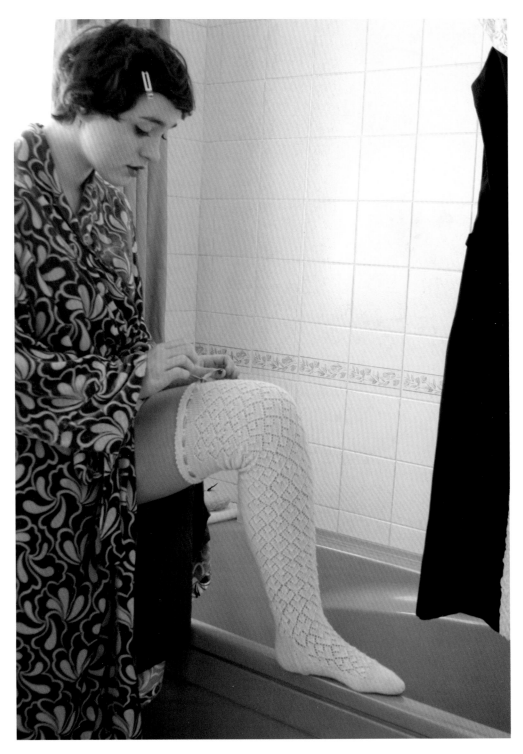

In olden days a glimpse of stocking was looked on as something shocking ...

Seamed Stockings

These elegant lacy stockings are knitted in 2 ply pure wool, making them perfect for everyday wear. The heart shaped motifs are complemented by a stylish seam running down the centre back of the stocking. With discreet leg shaping the stocking hugs and flatters the wearer. There is also charming shaping detail worked on the heel creating a 'fully fashioned' appearance to the heel.

These stockings would also make a spectacular gift to a bride to be to wear on her wedding day and beyond.

MATERIALS

Patons Fairytale Dreamtime 2 ply 100% pure new wool (approx 340 gm/ 370 yds per 50 gm ball) – this is a standard 2 ply (laceweight) yarn.
3 balls (one colour only – natural)
2 mm (US 0) dpns
Approx 3 m (3 yds) of 6 mm (¼ inch) wide ribbon
Stitch Markers

TENSION

2 pattern repeats to 5.75 cm (2.25 inches) using 2 mm (US 0) needles
Standard tension for this yarn is 36 sts & 48 rows = 10 cm (4 inches) using 2.75 mm (US 2) needles over stocking stitch.

This pattern is available in 2 sizes S–M and M–L. Leg length at different points can be lengthened to suit the intended wearer.

To find the correct size, stand up and measure up from your knee cap approx 10 cm (4 inches) and then measure around your leg at this point. Up to 45.5 cm (18 inches) you will need S–M, up to 56 cm (22 inches) you will need the M–L.

As the pattern is worked only part way around the leg with a stocking stitch panel at the back it is easy to increase or decrease stitches for the perfect fit. If increasing the stitches significantly add extra pattern repeats of 12 sts at a time. Each pattern repeat adds approx 2.5 cm (1 inch) to the overall width of the stocking. Extra decreases may have to be worked to compensate and to keep the fully fitted shaping of the stocking.

Our model is shown wearing the first size of stockings.

CO 121 (141) sts using 2 mm (US 0) dpns. Divide sts between 3 needles with an extra st on last needle. Join into round taking care not to twist work. On the first subsequent round knit this extra last st together with the first st (120, 140 sts).

Knit 10 rounds.
Next round (picot edge): * YO, K2tog, repeat from * to end of round.
Knit 10 rounds.
Fold stocking top in half with wrong sides together along picot edge. Matching each st, knit one st from the cast on round together with one st from the sts on your needles.
Next round (eyelets): * YO, K2tog, repeat from * to end of round.
Knit 14 rounds.

Commence pattern as folls:

Round 1: K25 (40) * K2tog, YO, K1, YO, SL1, K1, psso, K7, rep from * 5 times, K2tog, YO, K to end of round.
Round 2 and every foll even round: K to last 2 sts, YO, K2tog – this creates centre back seam.
Round 3: K24 (39), * K2tog, YO, K3, YO, SL1, K1, psso, K5, rep from * 5 times, K2tog, YO, K to end of round.
Round 5: K23 (38), * K2tog, YO, K5, YO, SL1, K1, psso, K3, rep from * 5 times, K2tog, YO, K to end of round.
Round 7: K22 (37), * K2tog, YO, K1, YO, SL1, K1, psso, K1, rep from * 5 times, K2tog, YO, K to end of round.
Round 9: K21 (36), K2tog, * YO, K3, YO, SL1, K2tog, psso, rep from * 5 times, K2tog, YO, K to end of round.
Round 11: K22 (37), * YO, SL1, K1, psso, K7, K2tog, YO, K1, rep from * 5 times, YO, SL1, K1, psso, K to end of round.

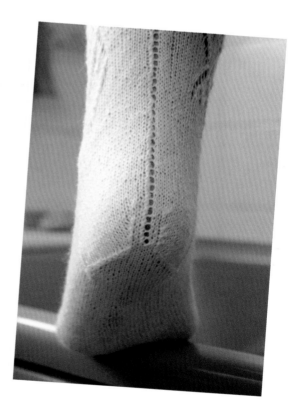

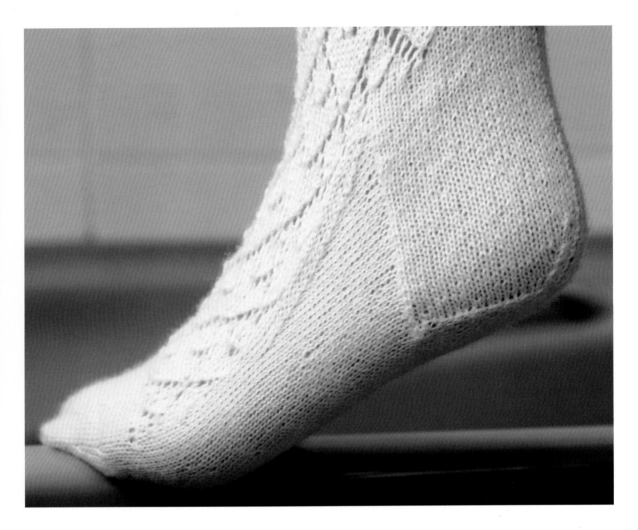

Round 13: K23 (38), *YO, SL1, K1, psso, K5, K2tog, YO, K3, rep from * 5 times, YO, SL1, K1, psso, K to end of round.

Round 15: K24 (39), *YO, SL1, K1, psso, K3, K2tog, YO, K5, rep from * 5 times, YO, SL1, K1, psso, K to end of round.

Round 17: K25 (40), *YO, SL1, K1, psso, K1, K2tog, YO, K1, rep from * 5 times, YO, SL1, K1, psso, K to end of round.

Round 19: K26 (41), *YO, SL1, K2tog, psso, YO, K3, rep from * 5 times, YO, SL1, K1, psso, K to end of round.

These 20 rounds form pattern. Repeat until work measures 37 cm (14.5 inches) from base of picot edge ending with an even numbered row.

Commence calf shaping as folls:

Decrease round: K3, SL1, K2tog, psso, patt to last 6 sts, SL1, K2tog, psso, K3.
Patt 9 rounds.

Work as for the last decrease round on every 10th round, a further 7 (9) times (88, 100 sts).

Pattern for approx 11.5 cm (4.5 inches) from the last decrease ending with an even row. (Please note, make a note of which row you are next due to work) Length can be altered here if required.

HEEL

Reposition sts on dpns taking 24 (28) sts respectively from each side of centre back for heel, leaving remaining sts for instep. Continue to work centre seam on every RS row. Work in st st until heel measures approx 5 cm (2 inches) or required length ending with a WS row.

Heel shaping: K to 4 sts before seam line, K2tog, K2, patt across seam, K2, K2tog, K to end.
Work in st st for next 3 rows.
Work heel shaping row once more. Work one row purl, then repeat these two rows twice more, then shaping row only once more (40, 48 sts).

TO TURN THE HEEL

Next row (WS): P17 (21), P5, P2tog, P1, turn.
Next row: SL1, K6, ssk, K1, turn.
Next row: SL1, P7, P2tog, P1, turn.
Next row: SL1, K8, ssk, K1, turn.

Continue as set, working an additional st before shaping on each row until 22 sts remain, ending with a RS row.

Next row: Pick up and knit 26 sts down heel, PM, patt across instep sts in patt, PM, K 26 sts up heel. You are working in rounds from this point (114, 126 sts).

GUSSET

Next and every foll alt round: K to within 3 sts of marker, K2tog, K1, SM, K to next marker, SM, K1, ssk, K to end.
Follow lace pattern on other rounds.
Repeat the decrease row a further 11 (12) times (90, 100 sts).

Continue in pattern without further shaping until foot measures required length. The toe measures approx 5 cm (2 inches). Therefore measure wearer's foot from heel to toe and subtract 5 cm (2 inches). The result is the length the foot needs to measure before commencing the toe shaping.

SHAPE TOE

Round 1: * K2tog, K8, rep from * to end.
Knit 8 rounds.
Round 10: * K2tog, K7, rep from * to end.
Knit 7 rounds.
Round 18: * K2tog, K6, rep from * to end.
Knit 6 rounds.
Round 25: * K2tog, K5, rep from * to end.
Knit 3 rounds.
Round 29: * K2tog, K4, rep from * to end.
Round 30: K2tog across round.
Divide sts evenly between front and back onto 2 dpns. Graft toe sts together. Alternatively turn stocking inside out and using 3rd dpn work three needle bind off across all sts.

MAKING UP

Darn in all ends, then thread ribbon through every other eyelet hole beginning and ending at centre front.

Arbour House
Publishing

Please visit our website at **www.arbourhousepublishing.com** for details of all our titles or to purchase a title visit our on-line shop at **shop.knitonthenet.com**

Abbreviations

alt	alternate		P2togtbl	purl 2 together, through back of loops
beg	beginning		P3tog	purl 3 together
BO	bind off		patt	pattern
CC	contrast colour		PM	place marker
cm	centimeters		psso	pass slip stitch over
CO	cast on		rem	remaining
Dec	decrease		Rep	repeat
dpns	double pointed needles		RH	right hand
foll	following		RS	right side
folls	follows		SL	slip
fwd	forward		SM	slip marker
in	inches		ssk	slip, slip, knit – slip next 2 sts knitwise then ktog.
Inc	increase by working into front and back of stitch		st(s)	stitch(es)
K	knit		T2b	twist 2 back
K2tog	knit 2 together		T2f	twist 2 forward
K2togtbl	knit 2 together, through back of loops		tbl	through back of loop
K3tog	knit 3 together		tog	together
kfb	knit into front then back of stitch		w&t	wrap and turn – slip st to RH needle, bring yarn forward, slip st back to LH needle, take yarn back, turn.
LH	left hand			
m	metres			
M1	make a stitch by knitting into back of loop before next stitch		WS	wrong side
MC	main colour		yb	take yarn to back of work (without wrapping round needle)
mm	millimeters			
P	purl		yds	yards
P2tog	purl 2 together		yrn (YO)	yarn round needle (yarn over)

About the Author

Susan Crawford lives in a seaside town in the North West of England, where she has spent many years working as a knitwear designer, knitting teacher and also lecturing in Fashion and Textiles. In 2006, Susan and her husband Gavin, launched www.knitonthenet.com, the highly successful online knitting magazine, and more recently, they formed Arbour House Publishing.

Susan is the co-author of A Stitch in Time, Vintage Knitting and Crochet patterns, 1920-1949. Susan's articles and designs can be found in many knitting magazines including The Knitter and Knitting.

A keen photographer Susan took many of the photographs for Vintage Gifts to Knit, assisted, when not modelling, by her daughter, Charlie. Susan's unique style and desire for authenticity can be seen in both the artistic and fashion styling throughout the book.

You can keep up to date with Susan's creative adventures and future plans by visiting her website at www.susancrawfordvintage.com or read her blog at, www.justcallmeruby.com

You can also follow Susan on her Twitter page @astitchintime

Acknowledgements

I would like to thank three people in particular, who have made this book possible. They are my husband Gavin, who somehow interprets my vague ideas and turns them into a reality, my mother in law Dorothy, who without question, knits, knits more and then asks for more! And finally, my muse and model, my daughter Charlie, who has become all my icons for me whilst modelling for this book.

Most of all, I would like to thank the editors, designers and knitters, usually un-credited, from my huge collection of vintage magazines who have inspired me by creating glorious knitwear that has stood the test of time.

Thank you.